T0342327

ADDITIONAL PRAISE FOR
PROSPECT RESEARCH
FOR FUNDRAISERS

"Too often, the partnership between fundraisers and prospect researchers is in name only. Now Helen Brown and Jennifer Filla have written a book to bridge that gap. No matter what level their experience, fundraisers and researchers alike will find in its pages a wealth of information ranging from organization and budgeting to data analytics and prospecting tips. This book will take its place among the few essential research reference books on my shelf."

—David Eberly, Senior Director, Prospect Development, Boston Children's Hospital Trust

"Often in the development area, we hear about the dangers of the 'Ready, Fire, Aim' approach, but Brown and Filla remind us that there is something that can be even more catastrophic to our donor relationship-building and that is the 'Aim, Fire, Ready' approach. We cannot start the process of cultivating and soliciting donors without first getting ready. This book provides both experienced development officers and beginners in the field with all the tools they need to get ready for those important donor calls. The resources provided and the real life stories of how to use wealth screening, anecdotal research, and other prospecting strategies to show the donors that you've done your homework, and that you have the donor's best interests in mind are crucial to success in fundraising. Congratulations to the authors on producing a book that should be in every development officer's library."

—Linda Lysakowski, ACFRE, President, Linda Lysakowski, LLC

"Fundraisers in organizations large and small will benefit from the insights in this book. Whether partnering with research experts or doing their own research, development officers who value information and understand how to gather, integrate, and use information from a wide variety of sources, including prospective donors, are more effective for their organizations and more highly regarded by the philanthropic individuals and institutions with whom they work."

—Ronald J. Schiller, Senior Vice President,
Lois L. Lindauer Searches

Prospect Research
for Fundraisers

The AFP Fund Development Series

The AFP Fund Development Series is intended to provide fund-development professionals and volunteers, including board members (and others interested in the nonprofit sector) with top-quality publications that help advance philanthropy as voluntary action for the public good. Our goal is to provide practical, timely guidance and information on fundraising, charitable giving, and related subjects. The Association of Fundraising Professionals (AFP) and John Wiley & Sons, Inc. each bring to this innovative collaboration unique and important resources that result in a whole greater than the sum of its parts. For information on other books in the series, please visit www.afpnet.org.

THE ASSOCIATION OF FUNDRAISING PROFESSIONALS

The Association of Fundraising Professionals (AFP) represents over 30,000 members in more than 207 chapters throughout the United States, Canada, Mexico, and China, working to advance philanthropy through advocacy, research, education, and certification programs.

The association fosters development and growth of fundraising professionals and promotes high ethical standards in the fundraising profession. For more information or to join the world's largest association of fundraising professionals, visit www.afpnet.org.

AFP Staff:

Jacklyn P. Boice
Editor-in-Chief, Advancing Philanthropy

Chris Griffin
Professional Advancement Coordinator

Rhonda Starr
Vice President, Education and Training

Reed Stockman
AFP Staff Support

Prospect Research for Fundraisers

The Essential Handbook

Jennifer J. Filla
Helen E. Brown

WILEY

Published by John Wiley & Sons, Inc., Hoboken, New Jersey.
Published simultaneously in Canada.

For general information on our other products and services or for technical support, please contact our
Customer Care Department within the United States at (800) 762-2974, outside the United States at
(317) 572-3993 or fax (317) 572-4002.

Wiley publishes in a variety of print and electronic formats and by print-on-demand. Some material
included with standard print versions of this book may not be included in e-books or in
print-ondemand. If this book refers to media such as a CD or DVD that is not included in the version
you purchased, you may download this material at http://booksupport.wiley.com. For more
information about Wiley products, visit www.wiley.com.

Library of Congress Cataloging-in-Publication Data:

Filla, Jennifer J., 1970–
Prospect research for fundraisers : the essential handbook / Jennifer J. Filla, Helen E. Brown.
    pages cm. — (The AFP fund development series)
Includes index.
ISBN 978-1-118-29739-1 (cloth); ISBN 978-1-118-41970-0 (ePDF);
ISBN 978-1-118-58548-1 (Mobi); ISBN 978-1-118-42157-4 (ePub)
1. Fund raising. 2. Fund raisers (Persons) I. Brown, Helen E., 1963- II. Title.
HV41.2.F55 2013
658.15′224—dc23

2012045892

Printed in the United States of America.

10 9 8 7 6 5 4 3 2 1

This book is dedicated to our prospect research mentors and colleagues. You are an inspiration to us.

Contents

Foreword

ROBBE HEALEY, MBA, ACFRE
Founding Member, Aurora Philanthropic Consulting

Think for a few minutes about things you like to do . . . but at which you will never be an expert. For example, I enjoy volunteering with my local Habitat for Humanity. In fact, I particularly like working on the sheetrock crew. There is something very satisfying about seeing the interior spaces of the home defined by the walls as they are finished. There is, however, no comparison between my speed and skill at hanging sheetrock and those of a skilled professional. The installation ratio of a volunteer to professional is probably 1:5, or more. The same ratio can be applied to prospect research.

We know we need to work hard and work smart. We are committed to good stewardship. We want to achieve our goals both in funds raised as well as managing the cost of fundraising. What do we do ourselves? What do we outsource? How do we decide?

In the past decade there has been a sea change in the way that prospect research is being applied in fundraising. Historically, prospect research has been reactive and largely considered to be a back-office function or service. Given the breadth, depth, and scope of information now available through multiple sources, prospect research has evolved. It is now a transformational springboard for fundraising success for organizations that invest appropriately and strategically. In this book, Filla and Brown explain concepts, strategies, tactics, and implementation plans in very understandable terms to empower fundraising leaders to make wise, cost-effective decisions.

As we've all experienced, technology and the way it can be used in development programs is changing quickly. Organizations that don't evolve and that resist using the latest resources and techniques will be behind the curve, or worse. As staff members on the front lines of technology, skilled prospect researchers are now full partners with frontline fundraisers in building and achieving organizational success.

That's why this book is so important. Filla and Brown clearly define not only what best-practice prospect research is but also discuss what it can do for you: how you can use research, prospect management, and analytics to your organization's best advantage and what the future may bring to a well-resourced department.

You may be thinking, "We have a subscription that finds everything we need" or "I just do a Google search and find everything I need." You are kidding yourself. Search engines give you the mere the tip of the iceberg; according to some experts it is only about 20 percent—or less—of available information. Subscriptions may give you a little more. But investing in research by a skilled researcher gives you a much bigger picture. A researcher pulls information together into a story with suggestions for donor-focused cultivation, solicitation, and stewardship. Their work frees you up to be out in the community where you belong, with your donors and prospects.

Let's go back to sheetrock . . . can you really perform? If you or your frontline fundraisers are attempting to do more than cursory research, it is not good stewardship of departmental resources. Compare salaries and think about who should be doing the research. Each frontline fundraiser, whether in a small or large shop, must be intensely focused on developing high-quality relationships with individuals and the interactive processes that will secure funding and meet goals. Organizational leadership may have a vision and plan for the future that requires expanding to a new level of productivity. Increased results are unlikely to materialize if we use the same behaviors. Using an expert researcher, either internal or outsourced, can be the difference between flat and growth—and is always more economical!

You may have met goals and even completed successful campaigns without research in the past . . . so why start now? Because competition is increasing, along with the need for highly segmented and personalized donor strategies. Success will require us to streamline our fundraising, target our best prospects, and stay focused on meeting donor needs. We must give each donor messages in the medium they prefer. Personalization can mean the difference between success and disappointment—or failure.

Peer reviews and effective discovery visits will still play an important role, but they are not enough. It is not reasonable to review and visit all of your potential prospects. Research can prioritize large lists and, especially prior to solicitation, complement anecdotal information with the kind of assets and giving history that rarely arise in conversation. Research helps identify hidden gems in our donor pool and frees us to focus on top prospects who have demonstrated that they are philanthropic. Filla and Brown provide recommendations for integrating research and frontline fundraising by helping us assess approaches, make decisions, and move forward strategically and intelligently.

Organized to make the book especially valuable both as a comprehensive overview and as a reference tool, each chapter includes a select bibliography of recommended readings and resources. In a style that is clearly written and easy to comprehend, these chapters discuss and explain:

- The ways prospect researchers identify new prospects, from simple to sophisticated methods.
- Individual, company, and foundation research, including small-shop tactics.
- Relationship management, ratings, prioritizing prospects, and reporting.
- Overseeing or creating a research department, including hiring talent, output, quality, and resourcing for best results.
- Ethics, risk, and due diligence.
- International prospect research.
- Trends and possibilities.

Particularly engaging, Filla and Brown have made liberal use of case studies, interviews, quotes, and tips that highlight topics and issues for additional thought or consideration. Each chapter focuses on a topic in such a way as to allow the reader to review and consider how to apply the topic to their shop and situation.

This book will be useful to staff at all levels of an organization. It provides a comprehensive overview, step-by-step guide, hints, and recommendations. It is the kind of book you will read, put on your shelf, and then refer to regularly as you meet new challenges and expand your practice. If you don't know where you're going, any path will get you there. We know where we are going and we want to be on the best path. Research can be our guide to the best route. Filla and Brown have provided the GPS.

Acknowledgments

Working in the fundraising field is a joy. This book would not be possible without the sharing, mentoring, and teaching our colleagues have given us over the years and continue to give. It has been our privilege and honor to be able to pull together our own experiences and the knowledge of so many people in creating this book.

We are truly grateful to all of the people who graciously donated their time for interviews and who provided case studies, expertise, opinions, and other valuable contributions to these pages. We would especially like to thank our colleagues who fearlessly reviewed our rough drafts and provided great insight: Jane Arnett, Chris Carnie, Molly Carocci, David Eberly, Susan Hunt, Marianne Pelletier, Sue Piergallini, Ann Satterthwaite, Ron Schiller, Allen Thomas, and Dina Zelleke.

Of course, without the AFP Publishing Committee and a nudge from Nina Berkheiser and Grant Martin, this book would still be inside our heads. A very hearty thanks to the team at John Wiley & Sons and to Becky Hemperly for the patience, advice, and support they provided to two new authors.

Lastly, but most importantly, we'd like to thank our spouses, Rich and Julie, and our close family, friends, and workmates who have shared our excitement, listened patiently, and provided moral support, tea, and sustenance while we wrote this book. Our deepest thanks for putting up with our temporary obsession, for helping to keep us sane and motivated, and for doing the stuff that we didn't have time to do because we were writing a book!

Introduction

Large institutions have been using prospect research since long before the Internet introduced blogs. Those institutions still lead the way in prospect research, but we have witnessed many different sizes and types of organizations harness the power of prospect research tools and techniques to enhance and grow their fundraising. You may be an executive director or CEO, a vice president, a development director, a prospect researcher, or some other fundraising role. If you are interested in understanding how prospect research can help your fundraising, then this book is for you!

Prospect research is a constantly changing suite of tools and methodologies that help fundraisers raise larger gifts in a shorter amount of time. To help illustrate this, here is a story based on real events and a very real gift.

Nancy, a frontline fundraiser with Midsize University, was attending the school's football game with one of her best donors. Patrick had made multiple gifts over the years and was very involved with his alma mater.

"Look who it is!" Patrick exclaimed. "Nancy, I want to introduce you to Sally. She founded a huge manufacturing firm that produces specialty fabrics for industrial and commercial uses. Do you see her? She's four rows down on the right."

"Yes. Wow! She makes quite a statement," Nancy replied. Sally was dressed up Jacqueline Kennedy–style, with a scarf around her head, big sunglasses, and red lipstick. She sported a classic 50s-style wool coat and spiky heels.

"I know. She's a bit over the top, but don't let that fool you. Sally is a shrewd businesswoman. It's just about halftime. Let's go over now."

Patrick introduces Nancy, and Sally says that she would really like to tour her old dormitory and classrooms. She has just moved back to the area in semi-retirement and is thrilled to be back on the campus.

Nancy requests the first level of prospect research for this newly identified prospect and conducts the tour. There is no doubt that Sally is capable of a million-dollar-plus gift. She meets with Sally two more times, but Sally hasn't been passionate about anything Nancy suggests and remains very reserved. A little confused about what to do next, Nancy stops in to see her prospect researcher.

The researcher listens to all of the things Nancy has been able to learn about Sally. She focuses her search on interests and hobbies and how she has been involved with other nonprofits. Bingo! Although Sally has not been recognized for a gift or volunteer service, she has made comments and been a guest blogger on a nonprofit website devoted to celiac disease. On the nonprofit's blog, Sally freely tells the world about how her daughter was hospitalized at 10 years old, losing weight rapidly and unable to eat because of the pain. Finally the doctors were able to diagnose her daughter with celiac disease. The researcher then searches and finds a professor at the university who specializes in the disease. She reports back to Nancy.

Nancy arranges for Sally to meet the professor and tour the laboratory. Sparks fly! Sally's entire face lights up and she is genuinely excited. A year later Nancy is at Sally's home walking her through the final paperwork for her first million-dollar pledge.

In this book we explain how prospect research fits into the fundraising plan and what impact it has on the gift cycle. We give you insights into the process with lots of real-world examples and suggestions. The book begins with the big picture. We illustrate how prospect research fits into your fundraising program and how to use prospect research to get more strategic in your efforts. Then we walk you through the traditional gift cycle.

This book isn't intended as a how-to guide for prospect research; there are several solid books, webinars, and associations for those who would like to break into the field. Reading suggestions are also included at the end of each chapter. We felt that an overview book for frontline fundraisers about prospect research—what it is, when you need it, and how to support its efforts within your organization—was missing from bookshelves.

Chapter 2 is all about identifying new prospects. You want to know how to find your organization's best prospects. Understanding the various methods available is key to making a good choice. You don't need to know every detail about prospecting methods, but once you have a grasp of how the tools work, you can shop with confidence and find a solution that fits your organization's target objective, organizational size, and budget.

Chapter 3 walks you through prospect profiles. You need information on your major-gift prospects that will get you through cultivation efficiently and effectively. You need confidence that the gift amount and type of gift you are asking for is appropriate and does not leave money on the table.

Chapter 4 is all about keeping your major-gifts initiative on track. Donor relationship management systems provide the structure for successfully reaching your major gift goals. Organizations that can systematically identify, cultivate, and solicit prospects for gifts are at an advantage.

Once you have mastered these prospect research concepts, it's time to consider what human and other resources you need. Chapter 5 discusses the different ways you might go about managing prospect research and Chapter 6 clues you in to the ethical and legal environment in which prospect research operates.

We also wanted to give you a sneak peek into where prospect research is headed. Chapter 7 discusses different ways organizations are pursuing international prospects and how prospect research can help. Chapter 8 highlights some of the newest software and methods with hints about where they might lead fundraising in the future.

As prospect researchers we get excited about data and research, but we are acutely aware that fundraising is all about people—donors, volunteers, fundraisers, and prospect researchers. Because of this, we have liberally sprinkled case studies, tips, quotes, and examples throughout the book. Also, included at the end of the book in the Appendix are ethical guides and prospect research skill sets from our favorite associations, the Association of Fundraising Professionals (AFP) and the Association of Professional Researchers for Advancement (APRA).

These days every book seems to have a website. This book does too. The site, www.Research4Fundraisers.com, is where we provide you with dynamic links, forms, templates, commentary, and the opportunity to add your thoughts and experiences and to ask questions. Prospect research methods and techniques change as quickly as technology—fast! We felt that a website, where we can add and change content easily, was the best place to provide you with ongoing resources.

CHAPTER 1

The Big Picture

If you've never come into contact with prospect research before, you may be wondering if it's something you even need. These days, most frontline fundraisers are pretty comfortable searching the web for answers to their questions and may be confident they are finding enough. Why should you spend valuable resources hiring or outsourcing something you could possibly do yourself?

You wouldn't be reading this if you didn't think there were reasons why prospect research is valuable, and of course you're right. Throughout this book, we will lead you through many of the ways research is used today and will show you cutting edge tools that will lead prospect research and fundraising into the future.

Let's start with the big question: What is prospect research?

WHAT IS PROSPECT RESEARCH?

Prospect research is the act of gathering, analyzing/interpreting, and presenting information that leads toward a gift.

Prospect research is a broad term that covers all of the activities employed in fundraising to identify and qualify donor prospects. It is not performed by one individual or a software subscription, but rather is a group of fundraising tools.

Following are some examples of prospect research activities:

- Searching online and offline sources for information about individuals, companies, trusts/foundations, government/municipal organizations, and other funding sources.
- Gathering information directly from donors and prospects.
- Methodically searching a donor database for donors and prospects who are more likely to give to an appeal, make a larger gift, or be a major donor.
- Creating lists for events or mailings.
- Providing speaking points for fundraising staff for prospect meetings and events.
- Creating and managing rating systems to prioritize donor prospects.

In general, prospect research activities fall into three main categories:

1. Prospect identification: Finding new prospects, either within or outside of your database, that have not yet been considered as prospective donors, volunteers, or advocates.
2. Qualification: Once prospects have been identified, evaluating factors to confirm that they have potential as funding or volunteer partners.
3. Relationship management: A system of directing fundraising activity by tracking progress through tasks and reporting. Its purpose is to move prospects toward a major gift.

Overview of Terms

Prospect research, fundraising research, donor research: These phrases all mean the same thing and are used interchangeably as umbrella terms to describe the activities involved in identifying and researching prospective donors, and managing the relationship between our organization and its donors. Even though the umbrella term is *prospect research*, the activity actually encompasses *research, relationship management,* and *analytics*. Most nonprofit organizations have one or more people performing each of these activities, whether they're aware of it or not. Let's take a look at each one.

On a very basic level, *research* is what happens when a potential new donor is identified and more information is needed to determine the strength of their linkage to the nonprofit organization, their ability to make a major gift, and their potential areas of interest.

Once a prospect is identified and determined to have interest, linkage, and the ability to make a major gift, the prospect is entered into a *prospect management* or *donor relationship management* system. (These terms mean the same thing and are used interchangeably). Very simply, a relationship management system is built to ensure that an organization keeps track of its relationship with each potential major donor. We'll talk more about the hows and whys in Chapter 4.

Analytics, also known as *data mining*, *donor modeling*, and *DMM*, involves studying the information in an organization's database to find new prospects. Analytics can be simple or very complex, and its usual purpose is to identify groups of prospects rather than finding prospects one by one. We'll speak in detail about prospect identification and analytics in Chapter 2.

As you can see, although the term we use is *prospect research*, there is a lot more to it than just the research part. Researchers are fundraisers—their work directly enables an organization to raise funds. And frontline fundraisers are prospect researchers, too—every face-to-face visit with a prospective donor provides an opportunity for primary prospect research.

Throughout this book, we'll be providing case studies, interviews, tips, and information to help you understand prospect research better. Whether you are a fundraiser in a small shop who wants to know more about how research can help you, studying for a CFRE and needing to know more about prospect research, or a chief development officer overseeing a department that includes research, our goal is to help you understand what prospect research is and how you can get the most out of it.

Let's begin by looking at the most fundamental question.

WHY DO PROSPECT RESEARCH?

> For a fundraising program to reach its full potential, those working on the front line—major gift officers, planned giving officers, corporate and foundation relations officers, and so on—must have a productive partnership with prospect researchers, whether internal (a prospect research office) or external (a prospect research consulting firm). Prospect research helps fundraising program managers make informed decisions about where to focus resources, especially time and travel of gift officers, deans and directors, presidents, board members, and others involved in the fundraising process. This makes the fundraising program more effective and more efficient.
>
> —RONALD J. SCHILLER, Senior Vice President for Business Development, Lois L. Lindauer Searches

It's hard to think about spending money to save money, but we do it all the time in our daily lives. Let's say for example that you decide to purchase a fuel-efficient automobile. You may end up buying a car that costs more than several others, but its fuel-cost savings and reliability rating means that you will spend less money over the life of that car than you would have for another.

Using prospect research is exactly like buying that car. Chances are good that before embarking on your car purchase, you would do research to determine the best features to meet your transportation, comfort, and lifestyle needs. You might purchase a subscription to a consumer's group website or magazine to give you access to test results and trusted advice rather than relying solely on brochures from the dealership. You may have made up a grid or used a spreadsheet to track your findings and rank your choices. Even though you can never know what the future will bring, you make your decision based on the best information available.

Prospect research is an investment in making the best decisions possible. Researchers identify promising prospects on which fundraisers concentrate their efforts. They purchase access to subscriptions that provide more reliable or deeper information than what is available solely through search engines. They track information in reports, spreadsheets, and databases to record data and decisions. This informed approach is an investment in personnel, training, and subscriptions (or in outsourcing) that helps an organization be effective and efficient at fundraising.

CASE STUDY

After a long period of cultivation, an alumnus of a midsize university was going to be asked for a gift of $100,000 to support the capital campaign. Before the solicitation call happened, the fundraiser in charge of working with the donor asked for updated research to be done so he would be sure the prospect had the capacity to make the gift.

What the researcher discovered was that the donor's privately held company had in the past month been awarded a significant government contract. In addition, the prospect's spouse had recently made a quarter-million-dollar gift to her alma mater in another state.

Based on this information, the team revised their target ask upward, and the $500,000 gift that resulted was significantly more than the original ask would have produced.

Prospect Research Informs Fundraising Strategy

We use prospect research to answer strategic fundraising questions. Consider how the prospect research activities described above answer fundraising questions:

- Who are our best donors?
- Do we have enough donors and prospects to reach our campaign goal?
- What is the best way to engage this donor?
- Where else is our prospect involved/affiliated?
- Is this company a good corporate citizen and potential partner for us?

- What size gift should I ask for?
- To whom should I send an appeal?
- Are we raising money efficiently and effectively?
- Is my organization moving our best prospects toward a major gift?
- Which trusts and foundations support organizations like ours?
- Do we qualify for local or federal government funding?
- Which of our donors are good planned giving prospects?

Without questions, we would not have research! Asking good questions and getting equally good answers provides many benefits to fundraising, such as:

- Focusing resources on the prospects most likely to bring the best results.
- Helping to provide confidence to fundraising staff.
- Helping us to get it right: the right person, at the right time, and for the right ask.

Research can be used to inform fundraisers about individual donors and prospects or entire campaigns. The following case study is an example of how an organization can be transformed through prospect research.

CASE STUDY

Liz is the new chief fundraiser at Cliffden College. Soon after her appointment, the board approves a plan for a major fundraising campaign, the college's first. Liz hires Bethann, a five-year prospect research veteran to help build the pipeline of prospective donors.

Bethann decides to hire a vendor to undertake an electronic wealth screening to help identify the college's best prospects. Because the fundraising database is rich with years of donor information, Bethann also uses her analytics skills to mine the database for additional groups of prospects.

Bethann and Liz use the information from the screening and analytics work, combined with firsthand information Liz gathers from trustees and key volunteers, to create a master list of best prospects.

Based on this work, Bethann and Liz are able to see the total potential capacity of their constituency. Using industry averages, they can use this information to project campaign totals and share it with the board. They track each prospective donor through their newly created relationship management system so that each one receives the attention he or she deserves and none are forgotten. Liz can use this system to see where individual donors are at every stage of cultivation and to forecast income by quarter or fiscal year for the entire campaign.

How Does Research Fit into My Work and into the Gift Cycle?

This is the key point that we hope you'll take away: Research fits into every aspect of the development cycle and, used strategically, cannot only enhance, but exponentially transform your fundraising results. Prospect research:

- Identifies a universe of prospective donors and volunteers to be pared down and prioritized through research and face-to-face qualification visits.
- Provides further information on the likeliest prospects and helps develop donor/volunteer cultivation plans.
- Tracks the relationship process with each prospect to ensure that each relationship progresses on schedule.
- Supplies key leadership and volunteers with information needed to assist them in making the ask for financial support.

Prospect Research in the Gift Cycle

Each organization's prospect research needs are different. Large organizations hire staff dedicated to prospect research activities. Smaller organizations might have only one prospect researcher, might have each of their staff doing various prospect research activities, or might outsource. Regardless of size or type, every organization has the same gift cycle. A donor may enter the gift cycle in different places, but the general process is constant.

At the center of the gift cycle are the donors and, from a prospect research perspective, the donor database. Even if your donor database is still on a spreadsheet, all successful organizations have some method for keeping track of gifts and other information about their donors and friends of the organization.

A visual representation of prospect research tasks combined with the gift cycle might look like Figure 1.1. Note that the ovals represent the traditional gift cycle stages and the rectangles represent typical prospect research tasks.

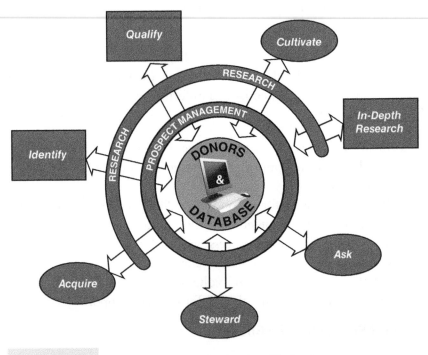

FIGURE 1.1   **Prospect Research in the Gift Cycle**

As you can see from Figure 1.1, prospect research touches nearly every stage in the gift cycle. This makes sense when you think of prospect research's central role in the gathering, maintenance, and use of information. In order for information to be useful, it must be presented in a meaningful format. Where does prospect research fit into the fundraising plan?

Now that you know what prospect research is, why we use it, and how it relates to the gift cycle, you can begin to see how it can help you increase the quantity and size of gifts to your organization.

Take a look again at Figure 1.1. Everything revolves around the donors and the donor database. Each of the prospect research pieces identified in the diagram support and enhance your ability to raise money in each of the main fundraising program areas:

- Direct appeals: Using prospect identification techniques, you can segment your donors and create messaging that is more personalized. You might also identify a group of donors capable of making gifts smaller than what would be considered major gifts, but at the high end of your direct appeals. This raises more money and lowers mail costs.
- Special events: Using prospect identification techniques, you can identify people to invite to an upcoming event or attendees of a recent event with the ability to make large gifts, and/or those who make gifts your organization or to others. Brief research on those attendees can provide talking points for your president and board members.
- Corporate, foundation, and government: Frequently having connections with individuals at these institutions makes these relationships most successful. Researching to find connections and identify interests and giving areas goes a long way to help you achieve success.
- Major and planned gifts: Major and planned gifts are the primary focus of this book. When you invest in the people and resources needed to identify, qualify, and perform deep research on individuals, your major gift program can reach new levels of

fundraising. The emphasis on major gifts in this situation is not just about raising more money overall; it is about creating an intense, personal focus on the small group of individuals who will likely give as much as 95 percent of your fundraising total.

COMMUNICATION

Good communication between fundraisers and researchers is important all the time, but it is especially crucial when there is critical information you need to know, there is a tight deadline, or the potential for wasting precious resources exists—for example, when going through an expensive prospect identification, screening, or data analytics exercise. Here are some tips for collaborating with a researcher on an in-depth prospect identification project:

- Meet with the researcher working on the project and provide them with all of the information you know and what you would like to know about the prospects identified or researched. Be clear about what you would like to receive back in your report and what format would work best for you.
- Come prepared with key words, phrases, donor types or groups that the analyst can use as a starting point.
- Discuss what your ideal prospect or prospect group would look like and why.
- Discuss your plan for involving and cultivating this new group of prospects; that may give the researcher more ideas about the types of prospects they should seek.
- Agree to a timeline for when the project will be completed and delivered to you.
- Agree additionally on a post-delivery meeting where you will discuss the successes and challenges of the project or process.

We all work better as individuals and as a team if we have buy-in to the process, a sense of closure, and knowledge of the success or failure of our endeavors. Prospect researchers are asked to provide information that informs a philanthropic approach but rarely receive the closure of that loop. Information that is helpful to ensure continued success includes: Was the information provided useful? How? How could we do this better next time? Did the project contribute to building stronger relationships with prospects? Did one or more gifts result from this work? Providing this feedback will enable you and your research team member to attain even greater success in the future.

DISPELLING MYTHS AND CORROBORATING EVIDENCE

Now that you have an idea of how research fits into the development cycle, we'd like to dispel a few myths and validate information you may already know:

1. *Anyone can find everything they need using that big search engine.*

    No, we can't. Measuring the amount of information available on the Internet is, at this point, like trying to measure the size of the universe. According to IBM, "Every day, we create 2.5 quintillion bytes of data—so much that 90 percent of the data in the world today has been created in the last two years alone."[1]

    It's expanding every second and it's a moving target. Imagine you're looking up at the night sky. What you see is pretty vast, isn't it? And yet it's only a fraction of all of the stars, planets, and galaxies out there. The information stored in search engines is *exactly* like that: vast, and yet only a tiny percentage of all of the information in web pages out there. And just like in stargazing, what you see may be current or may be refracted information from many moons ago.

    Free and fee-based subscription databases (like Factiva, Hoovers, and LexisNexis) are the telescopes that help us see deeper. They provide very reliable information, but they still only add a portion of all the data available. Primary (in-person or telephone) research can add another portion of information into

---

[1] "What is Big Data," IBM, www-01.ibm.com/software/data/bigdata.

the mix, which is why the information that frontline fundraisers add is critical to getting a more complete picture of a prospect's capacity, interest, and likelihood to give.

2. *Can prospect research tell me someone's net worth, or exactly how much to ask a donor for?*

No on both scores. Net worth is calculated by subtracting someone's liabilities from their assets. Since prospect researchers can only see assets that are publicly available, they will never be able to provide a net worth figure.

Researchers can discover (in many cases) major gifts that a prospect has given to other organizations or provide an estimated gift ask amount based on wealth factors. The product of this research is a strong factor to be considered—just as longevity of the relationship and depth of involvement are—in determining the right gift ask amount.

3. *I can do prospect research on my own; I don't need to pay someone else to do this for me.*

This is true; you don't need to have a researcher on staff or hire a consultant to help you. And when you're out on a call visiting with a prospect, you are doing primary prospect research. The more time a fundraiser sits in front of his or her computer doing research, though, the less time he or she is interacting with donors. What are your annual targets and responsibilities, and how much is your time worth? It's likely that a researcher's time is less expensive than a frontline fundraiser's and that their expertise in prospect research can get you the answers you need more efficiently.

SUMMARY

Prospect research is a great strategic tool to have in your development office's toolbox. But just as you wouldn't use a hammer to saw a board, research isn't the perfect tool in every situation, and sometimes it can miss the mark. If you understand research's value and limitations, using this power tool can help catapult your fundraising efforts from just getting by to substantially succeeding.

Prospect research gathers, analyzes and interprets, and presents information that leads an organization to stronger relationships with philanthropic partners and increased income. Fundraising asks the questions and prospect research answers those questions. It is up to you, the frontline fundraiser, to know what strategic questions you want to have answered. Do you need to know what size gift a prospect could possibly give to your organization? Do you need to find the most capable donors in your database? Do you need a system to keep track of your major gift prospects?

Although prospect research can benefit all areas of a development program, this book emphasizes individual major gifts. We wrote this book to give you, a person involved in securing support for a cause, a guide to the most important prospect research tools being used in major gift fundraising. We want you to know how these tools work so that you can make informed decisions about the following:

- Who fits best in the prospect research role.
- What role research plays in helping an organization meet its goals.
- Where prospect research fits into the gift cycle.
- Why research has been taking on an increasingly large role in fundraising over the past several years.
- How organizations are leveraging the power of research and its accompanying metrics to benefit their bottom line.

If you have been avoiding prospect research or feel at all uncomfortable around it, we hope this book gives you the kind of confidence that comes with understanding.

FOR FURTHER READING

Sonia Gilewicz, "Making the Case for Research," *APRA Connections* 23, no. 1 (Winter 2012).

"Measuring Fundraising Return on Investment and the Impact of Prospect Research," *WealthEngine*, May 2010, www.wealthengine.com/knowledge-center/whitepapers/measuring-fundraising-return-investment-and-impact-prospect-research.

CHAPTER 2

Identifying New Prospects

OVERVIEW: WHY WE IDENTIFY NEW PROSPECTS

All of the daily tasks we do to keep our nonprofit organizations steaming forward ultimately boil down to four critical and equally important responsibilities: identifying, involving, asking, and thanking donors.

Prospect research is one of the ways we achieve the first of those critical roles. We continuously identify new prospects because:

- We need our organization to continue to be healthy and grow in its ability to serve existing and new members, patients, students, and clients.
- Some people will lose interest in our cause or develop interests in other causes that take precedence in their personal philanthropic priorities.
- Loyal donors die and their places need to be filled by others.

We use prospecting methods to identify future supporters, but one other thing we're trying to do is minimize the annoyance we cause supporters with unnecessary mail, phone calls, and visits when they don't want them. It's good business to avoid irritating people, but it's also a smart way to save money, trees, electricity, and everyone's valuable time.

Both frontline fundraisers and prospect researchers are involved in identifying new prospects in a variety of ways. The process can be very low-tech, or it can involve sophisticated data-mining software programs and statistical modeling. Prospect identification techniques are used to find:

- New major and principal gifts prospects (individuals, companies, and foundations).
- Current donors that can be upgraded from lower-level giving to major gifts.
- Planned-giving prospects.
- People to invite to events.
- New (and future) board members and volunteers.

In this chapter we will highlight many of the most common tools and methods used to identify new donors. We will start with the simplest methods for prospect identification, such as easy data-mining techniques, and continue on to more sophisticated methods, such as computer-assisted data analytics.

We'll then discuss electronic wealth screenings and touch on list rentals, peer screenings, and surveys. If you are in a small shop or working with limited resources, you may find that you can undertake some of these simpler projects yourself; the more complex analytics will require both a larger budget to pay for the software or vendor's service and dedicated staff time to verify, analyze, and implement the results when they are returned.

CASE STUDY

When a major private research university began their recent campaign, they had 1,535 people identified as potential major gift donors. That may sound like a lot, but they had over $1 billion to raise to support scholarships, attract and retain faculty, and upgrade facilities and research capability. The fundraisers, both paid and volunteer, had serious work to do if they were going to reach that ambitious goal, especially since their previous campaign had raised just one-third of the new campaign's goal.

During the course of the seven years to follow, the university's prospect development team worked to update their alumni records, append a variety of consumer and demographic data variables to their records and strengthen their biographic and wealth capacity research methods. They used sophisticated screening and data mining tools to find people with the means and desire to make philanthropic gifts to the university. They modeled and segmented their data to identify new potential donors based on the characteristics of their current loyal supporters. They researched and fine-tuned the information to prioritize and raise the fundraisers' awareness of and engagement efforts with prospects deemed to have the highest potential to become major donors—and minimized fundraisers' attention on prospects with lower giving potential.

So What Happened?

- The research team identified 5,284 new major gift prospects, a huge increase over precampaign levels.
- The university received over $700 million in new gifts and pledges from those newly identified and upgraded prospects; nearly three-quarters of the total campaign goal came from these new donors.
- Fifty percent of donors who made gifts of $100,000+ during the campaign were making their first major gift ever.
- Twenty-three percent of the donors who made gifts between $100,000 and $5 million during the campaign made their first gift ever to the institution.

The university reached its original goal 18 months early and, during the worst recession of our lifetimes, went on to garner over $1.6 billion in total support by the time they concluded the campaign.

Can Their Success Be Yours?

Yes! This university is a huge organization with strong resourcing for prospect development. But the techniques they used

(Continued)

can be applied to your nonprofit and scaled to your needs. What are the building blocks?

- A cause that provides measurable results and inspires loyal support
- A multifaceted prospect identification program
- Policies and metrics for prospect relationship management
- Highly skilled prospect researchers/analysts who are both strategists and tacticians
- Effective collaboration between the research team and front-line fundraisers
- Inspired and engaging fundraisers (paid and volunteer) and leadership (paid and volunteer)
- Effective donor engagement and stewardship

Even a small organization with a staff of one can get the help they need to do this.

CAPTURING AND MAINTAINING CONSTITUENT INFORMATION

It can't be overstated: Every successful organization has a robust database as its foundation. By "robust," we don't necessarily mean huge or expensive. We mean a collection of information on its donors and friends—its constituents—that is entered consistently and with as much detail as is needed to fulfill the organization's reporting needs.

Consistency in data entry and the ability to retrieve information in a useful format are critical or else the database simply becomes a repository for a lot of interesting information that no one can access.

Having accurate and rich data is important for many reasons, but here are five to get started:

1. It is impossible to create relationships with people and ask them for philanthropic support if you can't contact them.

2. The more information you have, the more sophisticated reporting and prospect identification projects you can do.

3. Having good data saves staff from spending time trying to make appointments with donors who are uninterested or are not good prospects.

4. It gives you a realistic picture of your success in reaching fundraising goals and allows you to hone in on areas that need more attention.

5. It's the law: If you send out bulk mailings, keeping the addresses in your database current is required. Even if your organization is headquartered outside of the United States, if you send fundraising letters within the United States you may still be required to conform to the U.S. Postal Service's address update requirements.

Good data maintenance practices (also referred to as "data hygiene") are critical to your ability to raise money. Let's look at a case study that illustrates why data hygiene matters.

CASE STUDY

Mary worked as the sole data records clerk at the Rockland Community College Foundation for 27 years. During that time she entered every donor record and every gift into the organization's succession of databases. Mary never created a process document to track the way she entered information because she was the only one who did the job and it seemed a waste of her time.

Upon Mary's retirement, Sarah took over Mary's duties. Sarah was unaware of Mary's system of recording gifts and created new systems and codes to track the accounts in a way that made sense to her.

Sarah entered new donor information carefully, but when she was inundated with work she sometimes left off what she

(Continued)

considered extraneous information, such as a donor's degree or business information.

Everything seemed to be working out for the most part until it was time to publish the annual report of donors at the end of the year. Sarah's supervisor found that spouses were not credited with joint gifts. Donors with the same name were credited with gifts they did not make because their degree year and company affiliation had not been entered. Some gifts were credited to the wrong designation because coding had been changed. It all became a reporting nightmare that took months to untangle.

As the case study demonstrates, careful attention to the data in your database is vital. There are many ways to tackle a messy database. The long-term solution is to develop good habits and document policies. If you have a mess to clean up, you might consider the following possibilities:

- Contact your database vendor and explain the problem. They know their software best and may have a very affordable clean-up service, especially for things like duplicate records, bad addresses, and so on.
- Search for consultants who specialize in your database software. Talk to some of their customers about how the consultant helped them.
- Hire a talented database manager and/or invest in additional training for an existing employee.
- Clarify who should be entering information into your database and create documentation about how your organization wants it done.
- Work with your direct mail vendor to clean up you mailing lists and get the cleaned-up information back into your database.

How Much Information Do You Capture on Each of Your Constituents?

Data consistency is important for tracking information well year-on-year, but it's useful for other reasons, too. For data-mining purposes, the more information you capture about the people in your database—including job titles, spouse details, information about children, contact report data, and so forth—the better. Not only will your reporting and prospecting become more robust, segmentation for annual fund and membership appeals will become more intelligently targeted and fiscally efficient.

That's not to say that an organization can't manage with just the basic, legally required information. You can still find prospective donors in your database with just a few pieces of information, but if you have the staff and time to capture and maintain more detailed information about your donors and prospects, it makes good sense to do it. The key is to know how much time you have and what information is important for you to track and then stick to maintaining those elements successfully.

Basic Prospect Identification Terms

Now that we've covered the importance of having a rich database of information, let's talk about ways to mine that information to find new prospective donors for fundraising.

Many people use the terms *screening, prospecting, prospect identification*, and *wealth screening* interchangeably, and there's really no right or wrong term as long as you are consistent in the terms you use within your own shop. It's also important to be clear with vendors or out-sourced researchers on your expectations so that you get the results you pay for.

The most important thing, though, is to be clear in your own mind (or within your team) what the purpose of the project is and what you hope to get out of it.

HELPFUL HINT: SOME QUESTIONS TO ASK BEFORE YOU GET STARTED

Having a clear idea of what you want to accomplish before you start will set you on the path to getting the answers you need. Here are a few questions to ask yourself before you get started on any kind of prospecting project.

1. What do we need to accomplish with this prospecting project? (A clear answer to this question will usually tell you what type of prospecting project you will need to embark on.)
2. How many prospects do we need? At what level?
3. Do we have a plan for involving newly identified prospects?
4. How many new prospects do we have the staff/time to manage?
5. How much information do we need about each prospect?
6. What is our budget for this project?
7. Who will do the work or oversee the project?

The answers to these questions will help you determine the type of prospecting project that you will do; each type satisfies different needs.

Prospecting Project Types

For the purposes of consistency in this book, let's go over the basic terms. We'll cover each one in more detail in a minute.

Manual Screening or Manual Prospecting Project   A project normally involving reviewing or creating a list of prospects one by one. You might do a manual screening if your database is too small to justify the cost of an electronic screening or if you need to identify only a few prospects for a specific project.

What a manual screening might look like: A school based in the United Kingdom has a database of 100 alumni living in the United States. The cohort is perhaps too small to justify the expense of an electronic screening so the school outsources the research to a U.S.-based prospect research consultant to scan through the list on a name-by-name basis to identify prospects living in wealthy zip codes.

What a manual prospecting project might look like: An arts-based organization in Denver is planning an event to honor its retiring board chairman, a healthcare company CEO. The organization's research team searches through lists of the chairman's industry colleagues and business associates for people to invite to the event.

Electronic Screening   Data is electronically appended or added to an organization's donor file from a vendor that is contracted to provide access to wealth, philanthropy, business, and other information. Terms you may also hear include *wealth screening*, *donor screening*, and *prospect screening*.

An electronic screening, simplified: Donor records are downloaded from your database and sent off to a vendor. The vendor matches the names and addresses in your database to wealth and other demographic data that they lease or own. Your data is returned with the vendor's information added to each record. This information may then be verified, sorted, and analyzed by a member of your team or an outsourced researcher.

Peer Screening   A peer screening adds to the information known about a prospective donor or volunteer, usually by a person who knows them well. This could be a peer in their geographic area, class year, industry, house of worship, fraternal organization, and so on. Information from peer screenings is ideally collected and uploaded into the organization's database for future mining.

A peer screening example: Pat, a fundraiser from a small liberal arts college, is visiting Jim, a well-connected alumnus in Philadelphia. Pat shows Jim a list of his classmates in the area to learn more about them, such as their capacity to make a major gift and potential areas of interest at the college.

Surveying   Surveying entails providing a hardcopy or electronic survey to all or a portion of an organization's constituency to gather information directly from them.

Data Mining Data mining refers to pulling out useful bits of information from an organization's database. Data mining can be simple or more complex, as well as manual or computer-assisted. It may involve information from a database only or include previously appended data. Other terms you may have heard include *prospecting, analytics, clustering,* and *segmenting.*

For example: Mike decides to download a report from his organization's database that includes everyone who has made a donation of $1,000+ and who has the title "president" or "owner."

Another example: Emma downloads a long list of donors with their giving and demographic information. Using a spreadsheet program, she assigns points based on the presence of particular information in each record (title, degree type, zip code, etc.). She then ranks prospects based on their score and uses that as a starting point to begin further research.

Donor Modeling Donor modeling means using information previously gathered through data mining to identify new donors that match the same characteristics. Other terms you might hear include *analytics, regression,* and *statistical analysis.*

An example: Having established through data mining that donors aged 50 to 55 with a degree in business administration who are living in 20 specific zip codes are amongst a community college's top donors, Marianne uses a software program to see who else in the college's donor and non-donor pool matches those criteria.

List Rental List rental entails renting or trading a mailing list from another nonprofit organization or from a list rental company for the purpose of acquiring new donors or members. Lists might contain individuals that subscribe to specific magazines or aggregated by wealth band, interests, or a wide variety of other demographic elements.

MANUAL PROSPECT IDENTIFICATION METHODS

Manual prospect identification projects are called this because prospects are often discovered one by one or in small groups rather than as casts of thousands. The person researching might scan newspaper articles or investigate leads from a wealth list or "top ten private companies" list published in a regional business magazine.

These manual methods of research work wonders for brand new nonprofits, organizations who must reach out to the general community, or membership organizations trying to broaden their support, but they are used by prospect researchers in every organization type to broaden community support.

Manual prospecting projects are time-intensive but often result in well-qualified leads. Prospects identified can be individuals, companies, or trusts and foundations.

When Might You Undertake a Manual Prospecting Project?

You might undertake a manual prospecting project when:

- You are starting up a major donor fundraising program.
- You need to identify prospects for a special project or initiative.
- You need to broaden the base of support in your organization's local community.
- You need to identify companies and foundations to support your nonprofit.
- You need to find new board members or volunteers.

What Are Some Tools a Researcher Might Use?

Some tools a researcher might use include:

- Online or library-based company or foundation directories.
- Online subscription services from screening vendors.
- Free and fee-based resources that track board and personal relationships.
- Regional press or city business journals and magazines.
- Company and foundation websites.
- Wealth lists, such as the *Forbes* 400 or *Sunday Times Rich List.*
- Search engines.

Manual Research Sample Case Studies

Let's look at some examples of how manual research could be used.

Identifying New Board Members: Branching   Chris is the new chief development officer for a community foundation. The community foundation needs to fill two open board positions. To identify potential candidates, Chris hires a consultant to identify 20 individuals that are well-connected (and well-respected) in the community, who have the capacity to make a major gift, and who have demonstrated that they are philanthropic locally. Chris gives the research consultant the names of a selected group of current board members who have said they would be willing to approach candidates on behalf of the community foundation. The consultant *branches* out through each of these board members' networks—their other board affiliations, school and university networks, and so on—to find individuals within their networks that match Chris's criteria.

Identifying New Committee Members: By Interest   John, a major gifts officer at a school of public health, must create and staff a new advisory board for the department of environmental health. Members must have the capacity to make a major gift. Since most of the school's graduates are working in the public health field, alumni are not likely to meet this giving threshold. John asks Tara, his school's researcher, to devise a prospect identification project that involves identifying successful local companies involved in waste management, alternative power, biohazard cleanup, and so on. Once a cross section of companies has been identified, Tara creates lists of company executives, board members, and major shareholders, and together John and Tara create a final list of candidates to approach for membership on the advisory committee.

Identifying Foundation Funders   Beth is a fundraiser for an arts organization developing a new initiative to provide educational programs for low-income children. She needs to find foundation funders for this new initiative. Beth visits a regional nonprofit support center that provides access to an online foundation directory. She develops a list of keywords and searches for foundations that state in their guidelines that they will support such initiatives. Beth also does a reverse search within the database of recent grants awarded to find foundations that have made donations in this area but don't explicitly state in their guidelines that this is a priority. Once she has a solid list, Beth visits the websites of each of her top prospects to be sure that the foundation's funding priorities haven't changed, and to see if she can find personal connections to any of the foundation's officers, board members, or directors within her own volunteer leadership.

City business journals may publish salary surveys, lists of top companies or earners in a region, or top stockholders in local companies. Small, local newspapers may have a special section that lists real estate transactions over $1 million in the past week. Get to know local or specialized publications that may provide valuable information for your prospecting!

WEALTH SCREENINGS

Wealth screenings are the most common form of prospect identification conducted these days. They involve downloading specific fields from your donor database into a file and sending it off to a vendor. The vendor adds, or appends, external data to your data from third-party sources and then sends them back to you, usually in some sort of proprietary software framework like a database that the vendor provides.

Optional or additional services may include ranking or scoring of the returns based on assets found; a gift rating and/or propensity-to-give rating system; data modeling or other analytics; or refreshment re-screenings of the data within a certain time period.

> HELPFUL HINT: WHEN MIGHT YOU DECIDE TO DO
> A WEALTH SCREENING?

- If your organization is just starting or rebuilding a professional-ized fundraising program.
- If you don't know much about the capacity of your donor base.
- To help determine the feasibility of a capital- or project-based campaign.
- On an ongoing basis, to find prospects among new parents, new members, new admissions to your healthcare organization, and so on.

What Kinds of Information Do Wealth-Screening Vendors Provide?

The amount and depth of information provided by each vendor varies, but most wealth-screening vendors offer the data types shown in Table 2.1.

Preparing for a Wealth Screening

How you prepare for an electronic screening can mean the difference between getting good information to take your fundraising program forward and wasting a lot of time and money. There are four key elements to getting the most out of a screening:

1. Setting the purpose and goal for the screening.
2. Selecting a screening product.
3. Data hygiene, preparation, and delivery to the vendor.
4. Verifying, analyzing, and reporting on the results.

Setting the Purpose and Goal for an Electronic Screening

There are many reasons why organizations undertake electronic screen-ings, and being clear on your goals for your next screening will help

TABLE 2.1   **Data Types**

Information Type	Who It Covers
Securities holdings: primarily stock and options of publicly traded companies	Company directors, 10 percent shareholders, insiders (CEO, CFO, etc.). Covers about 1 percent of the U.S. population.
Real estate holdings (handy for discovering multiple properties)	Property owners. Covers about 67 percent of the U.S. population.
Private-company information	Private-company owners, partners and directors. Private companies are the vast majority of businesses in the United States.
Foundation affiliations	Foundation directors, donors, and trustees.
Philanthropic donations	Individuals, companies, and foundations that have given to a nonprofit organization AND have appeared on a publicly available donor list.
Political donations	Donors to federal elections and campaigns. Directors of IRS 527 PACs.
Geographic/psychographic segmentation	Scoring down to the household level of up to 90 percent of the U.S. population based on zip code, spending habits, and surveys.
Biographical information (career, education, family, avocations and hobbies, corporate, civic and philanthropic board affiliations, club memberships, etc.)	Over 1 million individuals in the United States.
Deferred income/pension plan inclusion	Over 2 million self-employed individuals are covered.
Yacht ownership	Owners of yachts.
Airplane ownership	Those with pilot's licenses.
Cell phone numbers, e-mail addresses	Where available; this data set is growing daily.

you make the right decisions around this expensive activity. Here are some questions to ask yourself and your colleagues as you prepare:

What do we need to accomplish? What do we need to discover?

- Learn more general information about the people in our database, including where they live and what their lifestyles are.
- Identify wealth holders.
- Identify philanthropic giving and interests.
- Help segment a large donor database.
- Identify annual fund donors for upgrading.
- Identify planned giving prospects.
- Find company directors, or donors working in companies with matching gift programs.
- Find prospects with ties to charitable trusts and foundations.
- Add prospects to (new) fundraiser portfolios.

Who are we going to screen? Are we going to . . .

- Concentrate on a subset of our donor/constituency base?
- Do rolling screenings of all new records added to the database or people served (such as hospital patients)?
- Screen the entire database?

Who is responsible for implementing and acting on the results?

- Who is in charge of selecting the vendor?
- Who will verify and analyze the returned data?
- Who will make sure new names are assigned to frontline fundraiser portfolios?
- Who will cultivate these new donors?
- How many new prospects can our frontline fundraisers reasonably manage in the next year?

How secure will the vendor keep my data? Do their data sources match our ethics requirements?

- What precautions do they take to ensure that our data won't end up on a laptop in the back of a taxi?
- Do they have a secure file transfer protocol (FTP) set up for our use?

- Do the data sources that the vendor uses meet our ethical or legal guidelines? (You don't want to discover too late that you have uploaded information to your database that violates requirements.)

LIMITATIONS OF DATABASE SCREENINGS

Computer programs are dumb and have no capacity to make judgment calls; the screening will surely match assets and other information incorrectly to people with the same name. In addition:

- You will incorrectly match 25-year-olds to $1-million houses if the address you hold is the student's when they lived with Mom and Dad. Electronic screenings only match the data they are given.
- Assets held in trusts will not be found. Many high-net-worth individuals put real-estate, private-company, and commercial assets (and just about anything else that has value) in trust, and these assets will not be found by an electronic screening.
- Co-op apartment owners are frequently attributed with the value of the entire building in a screening match.
- You will not find debts, credit card scores, well-hidden assets, bank-account details, tax returns, inherited wealth, or compensation (for most people). You will not discover if your prospect has two children in private school or if they have an immense art collection.
- If a person's address in your database is off by even one character, you will not get a good match.

Your board and volunteers will probably know more about their own assets and (probably) those of their friends and colleagues than will be found in an electronic screening. Consider doing both electronic and peer screenings.

A screening is just one source of information, much like what is gathered in one personal visit. It's a lot, but it doesn't cover everything—like that Monet on the wall.

No one vendor or source has the whole picture, but each has useful data. Some may capture data elements (such as private company-reported sales) that others may not. Determine what is important to you and find a company that matches your needs.

Selecting a Screening Product

Each vendor takes a slightly different approach to the screening process. Some concentrate results mainly on philanthropic giving, others on wealth identifiers. Some are large fundraising consulting companies and others only do screening.

Most provide a web-based service where you can look up new prospects or refresh the information you have about the prospects you have already screened. Some provide screening results in a format that allows you to track and assign new prospects in a relationship management–type database; others allow you to integrate the information directly into your existing fundraising software or relationship management system.

In addition to the questions above, here are some further questions to think about when selecting a screening product:

- Does my current database handle prospect management adequately or do I want/need a separate infrastructure to manage the returned data?
- Do we have in-house capacity to manage the amount of information that will be returned? Do we need extra help for the verification and analysis process? Does the vendor provide additional services that rate or qualify prospects?

Self-Assessment   Once you have settled on your goals and the population you want to screen, it's time to select a vendor to do the screening. Regardless of which vendor you choose, you're going to get *something* of value back, but each organization's donor and prospect base is different. Here are some things to think about as you make your selection:

- *What does our constituency look like?* Stock holdings and private-company information may work well for business schools or universities but are not necessarily the best for fine-arts graduates, a largely female donor base, or a retiree population.

- *How old is our population?* Many vendors use the same databases but to differing degrees of depth. Let's say, for example, that a significant portion of the people in your database grew affluent through stock holdings 20 years ago but are now retired. It's important to ensure that the vendor's records go back that far to report on that wealth.

- *How much work do we want to do when the results are returned?* If you are a one-person shop, you may want to consider purchasing additional services (such as modeling) from the vendor to pre-qualify prospects so you have fewer prospects overall, but ones who are more likely to give. A medium or large development operation may do modeling for likelihood to give as well and use in-house research support or outsource to a research consultant to help verify and analyze a larger pool of results.

Do a Trial Run   Talk with at least three vendors and see a demonstration of their screening results and online products. Products change from year to year and vendors change the databases they screen against occasionally, so it's good to be informed even if you used the same vendor just a few years prior.

Most vendors offer a free sample screening of records; take advantage of this opportunity!

- Send the same group of records to each of the vendors you are considering. Within the records you include, be sure to send a group of at least 20 individuals that you know well (including yourself), 20 you know something about, and 20 that represent a cross section of each of your constituent types.
- Ask yourself how easy it was to put your data into the vendor's format. Were there any issues during this process? Did the data-return process go smoothly?
- Were there pleasant/unpleasant surprises in the results you got back? Which vendor provided the most in-depth information on the majority of screened records? Which provided the most useful?

While you are waiting to get the screening results back, ask for a week's free trial access to each of the vendors' online look-up services and do each trial simultaneously. On each service, look up a group of at least five individuals you know well (including yourself), five individuals you know a little bit about, and five individuals that you know very little about, but who represent a cross section of the constituency types in your database. Ask the following questions:

- How easy is each online service to use? If one (or more) is complicated, does it provide enough information to make the extra effort worth your time to master it?
- Which provide you with the information that you most need?
- If you are a non-alumni based organization, do you need to do a lot of list building from scratch? If so, does one or more of the vendors offer the ability for you to generate useful lists of new prospects?

Then, call each vendor's references! Ask them . . .

- How well does the vendor score in terms of responsiveness and customer care?
- How good is their training on how to use their product?
- What issues did the references have going through the screening process and how did the vendor resolve them?
- Why did they choose that vendor over another? Have they used other vendors previously? Would they use that vendor again?

Negotiate!   The more records you send, the more flexibility the vendor has to give you a better deal.

Basic Information to Send to the Vendor

Each vendor will have a format or series of fields that they require you to send, but most conform to the following requirements.

(Don't forget to send spouse names/records for screening as well!) Fields include:

- Constituent ID.
- First name.
- Last name.
- Middle name/initial.
- Home address.
- Home city.
- Home state.
- Home zip (five or nine digits).
- Spouse's first name.
- Spouse's last name.
- Spouse's middle name/initial.
- Constituent's or spouse's maiden name (if applicable).
- Constituent's gender.
- Constituent type.

Extra Information to Send   In addition to the vendor's minimum field requirements, each company also allows you to send data that will not be screened but that you can use for sorting when the results are returned. We strongly urge you to take advantage of this! This will give you an extra data-mining tool and will provide flexibility and depth of information to identify different categories of prospects. There are lots of different options for additional information to send, but here are a few to consider:

- Giving for each of the past five years.
- Total giving.
- Affiliation type(s).
- Membership level/status.
- Degree/year.
- Marital status.
- Whether the prospect has children. (Yes/No flag)
- Whether the prospect has included your organization in their will.

What additional fields might you find helpful later for sorting data and creating reports? Ask staff members and your screening vendor for suggestions.

Information to Avoid Sending   Here are some types of information to avoid sending:

- *Business addresses and post-office boxes*: These rarely match to vendor information. Save yourself money by removing these from your batch.
- *International addresses*: U.S.-based vendors do not include non-U.S. information in their screening services. Unless you have contracted with a vendor that specializes in international addresses, avoid sending this information.

If budget or time is an issue, consider screening just a portion of your database, such as:

- Significant reunion classes.
- Constituents that were previously lost and recently found.
- New patients, members, and nonalumni parents and grand-parents.
- New season-ticket holders, purchasers of luxury box seats, or repeat ticket buyers.
- New donors giving above a particular threshold.
- Donors in selected states or geographic regions.

Screening Verification and Analysis

Some organizations don't have the staff support to verify and analyze all of the results that come back from a screening. Others prescreen (for example, using modeling) to identify only a small list of prospects that is used to send frontline fundraisers out on the road for in-person affirmation of the resulting leads.

A deep dive into screening results isn't always necessary. But if you have never done a wealth screening before or if you need to identify a large number of prospects for a campaign, making a plan for how you will verify and assimilate the results into your fundraising plan is perhaps the most important part of the entire screening process.

Electronic screenings are an expensive undertaking under the best of circumstances, so it's really important to make the most of your investment. Here are some of the situations you want to avoid:

- The screening didn't give you the information you needed or expected.
- Your chairman/president looked at a few of the returned records and found serious mistakes or omissions, so the whole project got shelved.
- There was so much data that your staff was inundated and couldn't manage it all.

Good planning with clear goals and a solid understanding of the capabilities and limitations of electronic screenings will help you avoid these issues.

Managing the Inevitable Data Inundation   Regardless of whether you send 100 or 10 million records, you will be returned a large file of information—it's just a glorious fact of the electronic-screening process. It will help that you will be able to sort the results in a variety of ways and that you will be able to print reports on groups as well as individuals. Even so, someone will need to verify the records that are returned and begin the process of ranking, prioritizing, and integrating these new prospects into your prospect-management pipeline.

What do we mean by "verify"? As discussed, there are pitfalls associated with electronic screenings. Chief among them are false positives: assets linked incorrectly to an individual because that individual shares the same name as another. You're certainly lucky if your prospects all have unusual names, but chances are that your database will contain more than a few Smiths, Joneses, and Browns. For example, to be sure that a vacation lakeside home hasn't been falsely attributed to your Mr. Jones, someone will need look at property records to verify that the valuable property does indeed belong to him.

Do you need to verify each and every record? Probably not, but take the time to make a plan for the ones that look the most promising that you won't have time to verify in person now. This may include an invitation to the prospect to upgrade his or her annual fund gift or attend a cultivation event.

Demographic/Psychographic Data Appends

We mentioned earlier in "What Kinds of Information Do Wealth-Screening Vendors Provide?" that you can have demographic and psychographic information added, or appended, to your database as part of a screening. These types of information are combined to describe the behaviors and purchasing styles of neighborhoods, streets, and households. Sometimes a donor prospect is ranked numerically with a wealth rating; other times the vendor provides a descriptor of the demographic group the prospect falls into, such as "Empty Nesters," "Power Elite," or "Suburban Style." These descriptors provide an additional way to segment your database to identify prospects, particularly those who keep their asset cards close to their chests, such as people who own privately held companies, have their home and other assets in trust, or donate through a donor-advised fund.

Risk and Electronic Screenings

Some vendors have the ability to append information such as cell-phone numbers and e-mail addresses to screening results. While these can be attractive options, be prepared to answer your newly contacted prospect's question "Just how did you get this cell-phone number/e-mail address?" Is the value of that information worth the risk of offending a prospective donor?

Peer Screenings

Discovering information about a prospect directly from his peers and colleagues is the simple principal of a peer screening. The frontline fundraiser goes directly to a prospect's "peer" to learn more about the prospect and his social, familial, and business networks. As you can imagine, this technique can be greatly rewarding but also has its pitfalls. Assurances of confidentiality and sensitivity are paramount in order to ensure that volunteers are comfortable in sharing what they know. Also, the peers selected must be a reliable source of information. Peer screenings provide insider information that is difficult for prospect researchers to find and can also provide a significant opportunity to steward a volunteer into an organization's "inner circle."

> **HELPFUL HINT: WHEN MIGHT YOU UNDERTAKE A PEER SCREENING?**

- In the beginning of a capital- or project-based campaign.
- On an ongoing basis, to identify new prospects.
- As an opportunity to cultivate and involve a volunteer.

Sample Projects a Researcher Might Do   Examples of a few projects for which a researcher might use peer screenings include:

Learn more about alumni in a class year or degree program: A researcher may sort an alumni–based list by class year or degree program. The researcher or frontline fundraiser would then ask a volunteer to scan through the list to identify any alumni she knows well to learn more about those prospects' careers and family histories, involvement in other organizations, potential interest areas in the school, and so on.

Learn more about leaders in an industry: If a database has individuals coded with involvement in a particular company or industry, a researcher may create a list of prospects by industry code or by company name in a city/state/region. These names may then be shared with volunteers in that region, industry, class year, and so on to see if they have information to share and a willingness to help involve the newly identified prospects.

SURVEYING

One of the best ways to gain information about a donor or prospect is to ask them. Surveys provide an efficient and cost-effective way of doing this and—in addition to biographic/demographic information—give insights we can't find anywhere else: a donor's propensity to give and his areas of interest in your organization. You can target surveys specifically to different types of people in your database, tailor them to gather different types of information, and test them to see which survey or delivery method works best. Don't assume that you already know the motivations and interest of your closest volunteers—you may be surprised at what you learn! Surveys can be developed in-house collaboratively between frontline fundraisers, researchers, and the department responsible for data entry. Or you may wish to work with a vendor to take advantage of its specialized knowledge in this area.

HELPFUL HINT: WHEN MIGHT YOU UNDERTAKE A SURVEY?

- If you have never done one before or have not done one in the past three to five years.
- In the beginning of a capital- or project-based campaign to determine if campaign priorities resonate with your donor base.
- In the beginning of a campaign, to segment donors for cultivation by interest area.
- On an ongoing basis, to find out business, civic, and philanthropic board affiliations; spouse name and business information; children's names and the schools they attend; philanthropic interest in your organization; salary/net worth ranges; and so on.

- On an ongoing basis, to identify prospects and gain interest and propensity to give from within a group of new donors, new parents, new members, and so on.

Sample Projects a Researcher Might Do

Examples of a few sample projects a researcher might do include:

Survey new donors at an organization's "wow" gift level: Survey to discover their current business information, philanthropic interest areas in your organization and their motivation for giving at that moment.

Survey trustees and other volunteer board/committee members: Discover their priorities for achievement during their service on your board; identify their philanthropic interest areas; and gauge their interest in hosting a personal or industry event or introducing you to their peers.

SIMPLE DATA MINING

You don't need expensive analytics software programs to do some very useful prospect identification on your own. In fact, if you're just starting a major donor fundraising program at your organization, some basic data mining might be just the thing you need to become familiar with your donor base.

> **HELPFUL HINT: WHEN MIGHT YOU UNDERTAKE SIMPLE DATA MINING?**
>
> - When starting up a major donor fundraising program.
> - When you need to be sure you have identified all of the "low-hanging fruit."
> - When you need to learn more about the people in your database.

Sample Projects a Researcher Might Do

Examples of a few sample projects a researcher might do include:

Segment geographically and by giving: Depending on the size of an organization's donor database, a researcher may download a list of recent donors to a spreadsheet and sort them first by donation amount and then by zip or postal code. They will look for answers to questions such as: Do the largest donors live near or far from your organization? Are they clustered in specific zip/postal codes or spread out? Are they large donors because that is where you have spent most of your energy, or are there other reasons? Now find a list of wealthy zip codes (*Forbes* publishes one every year for the United States, and there are several links on this book's companion website for you to visit). How many of your donors live in these wealthy zip and postal codes? Are there events you can plan in these areas?

Find new prospects by job title: Whether your organization is large or small, it is important to consistently track changes in the job titles of the people in your database as best you can. To search by title, a researcher may first sort the records in the database to identify important titles such as chairman, director, owner, president, trustee, managing partner, and so on. Next, she may set up an alert or weekly report to be generated when someone's title is upgraded to any of the ones you have selected.

The "wow" factor: Every organization has a donation level at which a first gift for that amount creates a thrill. For a small organization, that gift might be $50 or $100; for another it might be $1,000 or even more. To identify prospects by the "wow" factor, a researcher may sort recent donors to find any that gave their first gift at that level. Next, she may set up an alert or weekly report to be generated that includes all previous non-donors giving at that "wow" level. This will provide an ongoing list of prospects to pursue. Now a researcher may take it one step further: What *cumulative* giving level creates the same "wow" for the organization? She may sort recent and all-time donors to see who fits into that group.

Consistent donors: To identify consistent donors for a planned giving mailing, a researcher might download a list of everyone that has given consistently over the past five years. The researcher would try to discover who is new to this group, and who in this group has increased his or her giving over the past five or more years.

Company donors: A researcher may sort an organization's donors, alumni, or friends by company affiliation to find opportunities for a fundraising challenge within a company or to determine if a corporate gift or partnership might be feasible.

ADVANCED DATA MINING

More complex data-mining techniques include scoring or ranking the records in your database based on one or more characteristics that individuals hold in common, and testing to see if those characteristics have a statistical significance in determining whether a person is likely to be a prospect. You can also use these types of analytics to be cost-effective in your solicitation techniques, increase direct-mail response rates, allocate staff more effectively, and increase revenue. Methods include "clustering" to find significant groups of people by geography, frequency of giving, donation type, and so on.

HELPFUL HINT: WHEN MIGHT YOU UNDERTAKE ADVANCED DATA MINING?

- When a larger base of donors is needed, such as before a capital- or project-based campaign.
- When you want to segment annual-fund prospects for upgrade.
- When you want to learn more about your donors' giving patterns.
- When you want to build gift-officer portfolios.
- When you want to identify prospects for gift planning.

Sample Projects a Researcher Might Do

A few sample projects a researcher might do include:

Testing frequency of giving: An organization may do a study to determine at what time of year your most loyal donors typically give. Do they give to a specific appeal? Do they support the same designation year after year? Understanding this can help you solicit donors when they are most likely to give, saving you money in multiple unnecessary solicitations.

Testing preferred solicitation methods: An organization may do a study to find out if and how specific donors or constituency groups respond to a particular appeal or solicitation type.

Assigning scores to identify major gift prospects: In a project like this, scores are assigned to donors to prioritize and elevate the ones that show a higher propensity to give based on past behavior. The higher the score, the likelier the prospect is to be a major gift prospect. Research by Peter Wylie, Joshua Birkholz, and others suggest that information in the following fields is significant: someone's formal name (vs. their nickname), age/birth date, home phone number, business phone number, marital status, spouse name, e-mail address, family information, past donation over "wow" amount, and so on. A score in each category is assigned to each donor based on the presence (or absence) of that data point in a field. See Table 2.2.

TABLE 2.2   **Assigning Scores: Simple Example**

Name	Age	Home Phone	Work Phone	Marital Status Known	Spouse Name Known	E-Mail Known	Gift Over "Wow"?	TOTAL
Ben	1	1	0	1	0	0	1	4
Sue	0	0	1	1	1	1	1	5
Martin	1	0	0	1	0	0	0	2

In Table 2.2, Sue would rank highest, with Ben second and Martin third. If other prospects scored a perfect 7, those would be the ones you would want to concentrate on first.

Testing participation: In a university setting, a researcher may test whether fraternity/sorority affiliation, student–body leadership, or participation in an organized sport was correlated with a higher likelihood of a prospect being a donor.

DONOR MODELING

Organizations can either contract an outside vendor or have an internal specialist for this type of advanced analytics. Many larger nonprofits with a database containing hundreds of thousands of records, such as membership organizations, medical centers, or larger universities, have specialized talent on staff to pursue modeling work internally. Methods include using analytical software such as SAS and SPSS, and terms you may hear include *clustering, decision trees, CHAID analysis, neural networks*, and *regression*.

These techniques are commonly used as a follow–up to some of the questions asked in advanced data mining. Once an analyst has identified characteristics of strong past donors, an organization's entire database can be searched for other prospects that have similar characteristics to these donors.

HELPFUL HINT: WHEN MIGHT YOU UNDERTAKE DONOR MODELING?

- In the middle to end of a capital- or project-based campaign to identify the next tier of donors.
- To identify planned-gift prospects.

Sample Projects a Researcher Might Do

Here is an example of a project a researcher might do:

Through advanced data mining, a university data analyst discovers that donors over 50 who were in a sorority or fraternity, who have a dual degree, or who have a spouse who is also an alumnus are very likely to donate major gifts. Using donor-modeling techniques, she searches the entire database to identify others with the same or similar affiliations.

LIST RENTAL

Regardless of whether you are building a new database of donors or if you have over a million records in your donor database, list rental may be used to increase your donor base. List rental works like this: In collaboration with a list broker and a direct-mail marketing firm (often referred to as a "mail house"), you identify one or more lists to purchase one-time access to. You prepare a mailing to acquire new donors and provide this letter or package to the mail house. The list broker provides the list directly to the mail house, which sends the mailing on your behalf to the households on the list you've rented. Anyone who responds to the mailing is yours to keep.

Because list rental does not tend to identify major gift supporters and the work of prospect researchers is generally reserved for major gift fundraising efforts, a prospect researcher is not generally involved in the list-rental process, especially if the annual fund department has its own dedicated staff. However, a researcher is a helpful member of the team that identifies appropriate lists to rent.

INTERVIEW: VALERIE ANASTASIO

On the Analytics Project Undertaken by the Museum of Fine Arts, Boston

In 2008, the Museum of Fine Arts completed a historic campaign, raising $504 million, the largest ever for a cultural institution in

Boston. To learn lessons about what worked (and didn't) and to carry their success forward, Deputy Director for External Development Patricia Jacoby asked then–Director of Research Valerie Anastasio to do an analysis of the campaign data. With the help of analytics expert Marianne Pelletier, they began downloading and manipulating data and uncovered information that surprised and delighted them, taught them valuable lessons, and laid long-held organizational myths to rest.

Question: What made you decide that it was a good time to undertake such a project?

Answer: A couple of things converged at once. This project came on the heels of a major fundraising campaign that lasted seven or eight years. Over the years we had put certain systems in place so that the data was captured in a way that was consistent and well-organized because we knew we wanted, at the end of it all, to see how well we did and what we could have done better during the campaign. Because it was a campaign, we had a lot of fundraising activity so we had a lot of data that we *could* analyze. And senior leadership had questions about the efficacy of the work that we'd done and wanted to be able to plan for the future.

Q: What did you hope to learn through the process? What did you actually discover? Were there any surprises?

A: We wanted to know how successful our attempts had been with certain types of constituents. What did or didn't we do well? Were there lost opportunities? If so, what were they? We wanted to be able to track if there was a link between how we were trying to interact with donors and if they were responding well to what we were doing—if we were meeting their needs. We also wanted to figure out how to retain new donors and keep them involved over time so that they'll be there for us in the next campaign. Figuring out donor retention strategies were very important to us, so we wanted to see what factors contributed to increases in donor engagement.

What we discovered was that we were, on balance, pretty successful at retaining donors and increasing them, but we couldn't figure

(Continued)

out why. Many of the significant "touches" that happened between the MFA and its donors happen through event attendance, and that information wasn't stored in the database but in offline ways; on Excel spreadsheets and other places. Visitor system information wasn't well-tracked and stored in the development database until the end of the campaign, so we learned how important it was to capture and store that information consistently in order to learn more about the significant engagement events in a prospect's life with us.

Some surprises were the points of "positive vulnerability" in a donor's life with us that Marianne found. There is a pathway that a person at the patron level follows, and we learned that if we were able to retain them as a patron past a certain year, that there was a likelihood that they would stay with us for life, and there were a number of significant vulnerability points along that pathway. We used that information to engage people more significantly during those periods.

We were also surprised to learn from Marianne that there was a pocket of very wealthy people who truly believed in our mission and were strong supporters, but who were simply not interested in following the traditional major-gifts engagement strategy of being cultivated by a field officer. Once we realized what the characteristics were for that type of person, we were able to develop a meaningful way of engaging them that did not involve them spending a lot of their time at dinners or events they had no interest in or time to attend.

Q: What tools did you use?

A: In house, we used our relational database and Crystal Reports, which is a third-party application that allowed us to pull information from our database's tables into a format other software programs [could support]. We then used Excel and created pivot tables. Marianne used SPSS for her portion of the analysis.

Q: Can analytics be useful and affordable for a small-to-midsize nonprofit?

A: Absolutely, but only if you have a robust data set and can set aside time and the manpower to do it.

Q: What is the biggest consideration for an organization thinking about doing an analytics study?

A: Being orderly in your data-capture practices and having enough historical data to be able to look back to see trends. You can probably do fine with five years of data, but having 8 to 10 years' worth or more will give you much richer information to see trends and inform future fundraising strategies.

Q: Can analytics help people fundraise better?

A: Well, it can, but only if people are willing to be guided by what they learn. You don't always learn what you think you are going to, and sometimes the results can be counter to your organization's previously held beliefs. It doesn't make sense to spend the time and money to undergo an analytics project and not follow up on the recommendations. One of the things that most people learn is how incredibly important good data-capturing procedures are, but it's an area that's generally pretty neglected. Good data is the lifeblood of an organization. It captures the relationship of a donor to an organization, which, we hope, is much longer than any one fundraiser's tenure at that organization.

SUMMARY

As this chapter illuminates, there are a wide variety of ways to identify new prospects and there are methods for every size and type of organization, from simple data mining to sophisticated statistical analysis. It is important to begin with a database full of information that is accurate and "clean." When your database is full of errors and missing information, your prospect–identification efforts will suffer.

In this chapter we talked about the following types of prospecting:

Manual Screening or *Manual Prospecting Projects*: These are ways to quickly rate a small donor list or build your prospect list by hand. This makes sense when you have a small, targeted list or you need to start a prospect list from scratch.

Electronic or *Wealth Screening*: If you have a large group of records and are trying to find your wealthiest and most capable prospects, an electronic wealth screening can be very effective. Information from the records in your database are exported and provided in a file to a vendor who compares them against public information and other sources. The match results—those individuals who have information attached to their names—are given back to you, often in a software format such as a database or Excel spreadsheet.

Peer Screening: Long before databases and the Internet, fundraisers asked people to rate their peers for likely gift amounts, interests, giving motivations, and other information. This is still an exercise that yields valuable information and provides an opportunity to engage with and ask the advice of key volunteers.

Surveying: Like peer screening, this prospecting method has been around a long time. Directly asking your donors and friends about themselves through surveys will give you information not found anywhere else.

Data Mining: There are many creative techniques for sorting the information in your donor records to identify patterns correlated with good prospects. A simple sort might look for the highest lifetime giving with the most recent gift date. You can also employ more complicated methods to get more nuanced or targeted results.

Donor Modeling: Like data mining generally, donor modeling looks for patterns that suggest a good prospect, but donor modeling uses high-level techniques requiring specialized skills and software. Because it most often involves statistical analysis, it requires a larger group of records—ideally 10,000 or more.

List Rental: Especially for organizations who have to reach out to the community to find donors and do not have a natural constituency (like a university has in its graduates or a hospital has in its patients), renting a segmented list of names to solicit for gifts can make a lot of sense. Many human services and advocacy organizations have used this method very successfully. Typically a prospect researcher is not involved in managing this kind of project.

Whether your organization is large or small, there is a prospecting technique to match your needs. Overall, when prospecting:

- Make a plan for what you want to accomplish and select a prospect-identification method that best suits your needs and budget.
- Allocate enough time and human-power to manage the project and its outcome.
- Be prepared for the frustration and delight that all prospecting projects produce!

We also discussed what impact the quality of the information in your database has on the quality of your fundraising. This impact deepens as the number of your donors grows. Whatever size organization you work for, it is a good time to review your database usage. Without consistent data entry and solid reporting, you risk damaging all of your fundraising efforts. For example, duplicate donor records leads to erroneous gift reporting. Don't underestimate, or underinvest in, the quality of your data!

FOR FURTHER READING

Birkholz, Joshua. *Fundraising Analytics: Using Data to Guide Strategy*. Hoboken, NJ: John Wiley & Sons, 2008.
Hart, Ted, James M. Greenfield, Pamela M. Gignac, and Christopher Carnie. *Major Donors: Finding Big Gifts in Your Database and Online*. Hoboken, NJ: John Wiley & Sons, 2006.

CHAPTER 3

Researching Prospects

One thing that I would love for gift officers to know is that we love when they share with us everything they already know, or think they know, about a prospect before we begin our research efforts! Sometimes a small piece of information that has been gathered and shared internally is the golden key that allows the research team to pull together their findings and confirm x, y, and z about the prospect.

—JENNIFER FALCON, Director of Research and Prospect
Management, Saint Joseph's University

Donor research is an important fundraising task that can be accomplished in many ways. The more complex your fundraising program and the more dollars raised, the more likely you will be to purchase resources and hire skilled researchers. However, take caution never to overlook one of the oldest and most obvious sources of information—face-to-face conversation.

- The donor who wants to introduce you to someone usually has something to say about why that person is a good prospect.
- Peer-review meetings with select volunteers elicit all sorts of valuable insights and connections that cannot be duplicated elsewhere.

- Conversations with your prospects yield very personal and private information, such as why they give and how they feel about your organization.

In addition to the tried and true in-person information gathering, there are now many other opportunities to gather information from the public domain that can give you an important edge as you aspire to work ever more quickly and efficiently to close gifts with your prospects. In this chapter we discuss creating prospect profiles, what types of tools are available, and search techniques every fundraiser needs to know.

Understanding the information that can be found and the tools available to find it is necessary for every fundraiser who needs to make decisions and build a fundraising plan. In our world of electronic technology and online connectivity, good online search technique is a life skill. Any fundraiser without basic search skills is at a disadvantage.

DIFFERENT LEVELS OF RESEARCH

In Chapter 5, "Managing Prospect Research," we talk briefly about creating a research request form and various donor-prospect profile templates. An easy way of discussing the profile types is to take a look at how prospect research fits into the giving cycle. (For this, you can refer back to Figure 1.1.)

This may sound obvious to you, but the closer you are to asking for a gift, the more time you should spend researching the individual. Why spend 6 to 10 hours researching a prospect who has never been visited to determine his or her capacity for giving and interest in your organization? It is much more worthwhile to spend that kind of time when you know the prospect wants to make a significant gift.

Many a prospect researcher has complained about a fundraising manager asking for "everything you can find" on a prospect that is not even known to the organization. As we explain in Chapter 5, defining research requests using a request form and talking with the requester can go a long way towards efficiency. But even if you have a defined policy for requesting research, there are always exceptions to the rules. For example, if the CEO has landed a meeting with a high-profile individual and it might be the only chance to ask for a gift, deep research could mean the difference between getting the gift or not. However, if someone hears about a business person on the news on the way in to work, brief research or looking first for linkage is usually a better choice than a full-blown profile.

TYPES OF DONOR PROFILES

Once we have identified our prospects, we want to know more about them. In particular we want to discover:

- *Affinity:* How close the prospect feels to your organization.
- *Capacity:* The prospect's level of wealth, or ability to make a major gift.
- *Inclination or propensity to give:* Whether the prospect makes gifts to your organization and other nonprofits.

If you are studying for your Certified Fund Raising Executive (CFRE) exam or have been in the fundraising field for a while, you might see different words being used in relation to qualifying a prospect. They have the same or very similar meanings. Here is how the terms stack up:

Frontline Fundraising	Prospect Research
Linkage	Affinity
Ability	Capacity
Inclination	Inclination

(Continued)

Linkage is the only term with a slightly different meaning. *Linkage* refers to how the prospect is or could be connected with your organization. *Affinity* specifically refers to how close the prospect feels to your organization, which includes how the prospect is linked. For example, a prospect may be linked to your organization as a long-time volunteer. This volunteer status would also indicate affinity. However, as a frontline fundraiser cultivates a prospect, he will look beyond linkage to how the prospect feels overall toward the organization. This affinity rating helps the fundraiser determine what type of solicitation strategy to pursue.

For convenience, in this book we name the profiles after the period during the gift cycle when we typically want more information:

- *Identification/qualification.* The point when a new prospect is identified and needs to be visited by a fundraiser to further qualify their interest, likelihood of giving, and capacity to make a major donation in the future.
- *Cultivation:* The period when a donor is involved in the life of the organization. Information gathered may be a combination of primary (in-person) and secondary prospect research.
- *Solicitation:* The period leading up to and including the ask for a major donation. At this point, the researcher is usually asked to find up-to-date financial and donation information.

You might find that different profile-naming systems and different levels of research may work better in your office. You may have other needs for information, such as event biographies or prospect briefings for leadership, or you may have other ways of organizing your profile types. For example, you might choose to name your profiles Level I and Level II and have another type for the president's briefings. This will all depend upon the size and complexity of your fundraising operations. Defining profile types based on your organization's fundraising needs helps you stay focused on what and how much information you want to find.

Individual Profiles

Regardless of the reason we are creating a donor profile, there are five fundamental areas of a profile representing key information used in cultivating and soliciting a major gift. Let's review each of the key areas first and then discuss different methods for finding information in each area.

Biographical   In this section you will find a person's current contact information, including their home, seasonal, and business addresses. Sometimes a photograph of the individual and their spouse or partner is included as well for easy identification.

We also want to know all about the person's family, hobbies, interests, and education. Family connections need to be understood, especially if there is inherited wealth. This section helps the frontline fundraiser make initial conversation and begin to probe for motivations and interests that could inspire giving.

Relationship to Your Organization   This lets the frontline fundraiser know what has happened most recently with the prospect. Usually included are board or volunteer positions held at the organization, a summary of giving, the assigned solicitor, and a summary of interactions or the last interaction with a prospect or the prospect's family. If capacity and other ratings are not included elsewhere, such as at the top of the profile, you will want them here.

Community Involvement and Giving   In this section you will find out if your prospect or her spouse serves on other civic or philanthropic boards of directors, and whether there is a family foundation or any giving to other organizations that has been reported to the public. Also included is whether the prospect's name or family's name is on buildings, scholarships, or endowed funds. A prospect may have an interest in your organization and enough wealth to make a difference, but if the prospect does not make gifts or volunteer, the likelihood of a gift drops precipitously. Spending time on this section can go a long way toward informing the strategy for future cultivation visits and, ultimately, the major gift ask.

Occupation/Career History   In this section of a profile you will find current and/or historical career information about a prospect, including information about his current place of employment. Unless the family has inherited wealth, and even then, individuals most often accumulate wealth through an occupation.

Information availability varies greatly depending on whether you are researching public or privately held companies. If a prospect is a top executive of a public company, there is usually a lot of information available—even the employment agreement may be findable. For privately held companies, there may be a great deal of information or very little.

Sometimes, how the prospect feels about money is unveiled through nuggets of information found in this area, such as an interview or news article describing "how Clark Gable first learned the value of a dollar on his newspaper route" and how he now owns and runs a multinational company as a result. What you learn about a prospect's attitude toward money could completely change your cultivation and solicitation strategy. Should you steer Clark Gable toward an endowed scholarship, or will he name the new business school, or both?

Assets   Real estate, insider securities, art collections, airplanes, yachts, and other luxury items owned by the prospect fill this section of the profile. Through these accumulated assets we try to assess the scope of a prospect's wealth. Combined with occupation, assets are what we often rely upon to assess the prospect's capacity. Detailing assets is where we try to add more certainty to how much wealth there is and for what level of gift we may be able to ask.

Company Profiles

Company profiles can have many purposes. You may be considering a corporate prospect for a philanthropic gift or for sponsorship. Sometimes corporate research is done to determine if an individual prospect would be more likely to make a gift from a company than on his or her own. Whatever the purpose, following are some key elements that should be part of a company profile.

Contact Information   In this section you will find the company's main location and its address and telephone number. Other pertinent addresses, such as a local branch, could also be included. The company's web page, as well as any social media presences—like a Facebook page or Twitter account—should also be found in this section.

Company Description   The goal of this section is to understand what the company does, who leads it, and how it fits into its industry relative to other companies. The level of information will vary depending on how much detail is needed and whether the company is public or private, but in this section you may find the founding date of the company, the number of employees, and its sales and leadership information. Also included will be information about the company's products or services and its recent performance or other news and information that might affect the company's interest or ability to make a gift.

Company Philanthropy   Increasingly, companies are including information about their Corporate Social Responsibility (CSR) on their websites. This may include corporate donations or sponsorships, employee volunteerism in the community, and social or environmental impact statements. This information is very important to include on a profile because it leads us to the heart of the question: Does this company make gifts to nonprofit organizations? Has it made gifts to our organization, and if so, how much and for what?

You may also find that the company has created a separate corporate foundation. This corporate foundation could be the only way the company makes gifts or it could be in addition to other philanthropic activities.

Relationship to Your Organization   How a donor is connected to your organization is always important, and companies are no different. For a company, you want to know whether any of the employees, especially executives, are alumni, members, former patients, or have a past affiliation, or if they hold board or volunteer positions at your organization. You will also want to outline a summary of the company's giving; the assigned solicitor; and a summary of interactions or the last interaction your organization had with the company.

Additional questions that should be answered in this section of a company profile might include:

- Have any employees benefited from our services?
- How many employees has our college educated?
- Is valuable research done at our hospital allied with a company's interest, product, or service?

Foundation Profiles

If your individual prospect has a family foundation, this information is most often incorporated into the individual prospect's overall profile. But if you are focused specifically on the foundation as a potential donor, you will likely want to create a profile just for that foundation.

Contact Information   Included in this section should be the address, telephone and web contact information, and any program officers or directors who are or will be your organization's main contacts. If the foundation has a presence on Facebook, Twitter or other social media, you will want to include it here.

Areas of Interest and Limitations   In this section, you will find both the foundation's stated areas of interest and any other giving that the person researching the foundation has found. Many foundations give outside of their stated interest areas if they are testing new programs or following the philanthropic interest of an individual board member. It is important to look both at stated interest and at recent philanthropy to get a full picture of a foundation's scope of giving. Some more detailed information about grants awarded and motivations for giving could be found reported in the news, on the foundation's website or on their grantees' websites.

Also in this section, you will find specific information about types of organizations that the foundation will (or will not) support, as well as geographic areas where the foundation has an interest. In some cases, foundations indicate that they will give internationally or nationally; in other cases they are very specific on the states, regions, or cities to which they limit their support.

Recent Philanthropic Giving   Depending on how much depth you need to see and/or the size of the foundation, "philanthropic giving" could include all gifts over the past three to five years, gifts of a certain amount and above, or gifts to specific interest areas. Every foundation must report each grant made, to whom, and for how much on its IRS Form 990 tax form. This information is public and can be accessed easily and for free on www.guidestar.org or at http://foundationcenter.org.

Relationship to Your Organization   If you do not already know what connection you have to a foundation, this section should help you find a link. Especially when a foundation's application guidelines are very structured and formal, having a connection to an individual of influence at the foundation will be of help as you go through the application process.

Questions answered in this section might include:

- Is one of the foundation's executives or program officers an alumnus of your university or on your organization's board?
- Does a member of your board have a connection to a board member of the foundation?
- Is a foundation trustee perhaps already a donor to your nonprofit?

ASSEMBLING YOUR RESEARCH TOOLKIT

Once you have decided what types of profiles you need based on your current fundraising plans, take a look at the number of major gifts you hope to raise in a year, and then work back to how many prospects need to be cultivated to close those gifts. A broad rule of thumb is that it takes four qualified prospects to close one gift. By this metric, you might need four identification/qualification or cultivation profiles before you are ready to solicit one prospect, and will need one solicitation profile for every major gift received.

Assess the Scope of Your Profile Needs

Now that you know how many profiles you will likely need in a year, consider these ballpark estimates for the amount of time needed to complete each profile:

- *Identification/qualification profile*: 1 to 3 hours.
- *Cultivation profile*: 2 to 4 hours.
- *Solicitation profile*: 6 to 12 hours.

CASE STUDY

Chosen Charity has three frontline fundraisers who are each expected to qualify 50 new prospects a year, make eight substantial visits a month, make 20 solicitations, and generally manage a portfolio of 150 donors and prospects. They will need a prospect researcher to support their work with profiles as follows:

Fifty identification profiles: 50 profiles × 3 hours = 150 hours

Twenty solicitation profiles: 20 profiles × 8 hours = 160 hours

Minimum of 310 research hours × 3 frontline fundraisers = 930 total research hours (or nearly 27 weeks at 35 hours per week)

Chosen Charity decides to use an outside firm to provide profiles this year and budgets for the hiring of a part-time researcher in the next fiscal year.

Not only can this type of analysis help you if you are trying to decide whether to hire staff or outsource, it can help you make practical choices about how much you need to know and who will be in charge of finding it. Acquiring and maintaining prospect research skills takes time and training.

Fee versus Free

There are endless possibilities for combining paid and free resources. In Chapter 5, we provide you with some free and fee resources in three categories: search, analytics, and summary look-up tools. The online complement to this book, www.Research4Fundraisers.com, also provides a continuously updated list of resources.

Specific resources will be discussed next as we walk through finding information for each area of the profile. Following are two examples of combinations for a small (1 to 5 staff) and large (10+ staff) fundraising office to give you an idea of how you might assemble your resources for searching individuals, companies, and foundations. You might also want to review the real-life success stories at the end of Chapter 5.

Small Office Example (1 to 5 Staff)   Save the Pelican has three fundraising staff and an operating budget of under $1 million. When it fell short funding a project and asked a longtime donor for another gift, she volunteered to make up for the entire shortfall and any shortfall on that project in the future. It was then that the organization realized that some of their donors might have far greater capacity than originally suspected. When Save the Pelican wanted to update its medical offices for rescued birds, it identified 100 possible major gift prospects from its database based on giving amount, giving frequency, and giving longevity. Staff also received recommendations on new prospects from its board of directors.

Save the Pelican hired a prospect research firm to find assets, occupation, and other giving information as well as assign a capacity rating for all 100 prospects. It took six weeks to complete the project.

Together with the board, the fundraising staff rated all 100 prospects on what they called "interest." Prospects known to have an interest in the organization through demonstrated giving and volunteering were given the highest rating of "A," those with some giving were given a "B," and those with the lowest known interest or no giving were given a "C."

Now, armed with a reasonable prospect list, the staff cultivated their prospects and requested in-depth profiles from the outside firm as they approached solicitations of $10,000 or more.

Large Office Example (10+ Staff)   End Hunger Now (EHN) has 50 staff in its development offices. EHN has a director of research and prospect management as well as two full-time researchers. The research budget affords around $35,000 to purchase several fee-based resources.

EHN is about to announce a $50 million campaign to fund expanded programs, hire staff, and increase its advocacy program. To do this, the organization needs to assess its current donor pool to identify any gaps in its campaign pyramid, identify new prospects, and track prospects through its prospect management system.

EHN contracts with a wealth screening company that provides data analytics to assess prospect affinity as part of its services. Once the data come back, the top segment of previously unknown prospects with confirmed assets of $5 million and above is swiftly double-confirmed by the research staff. Each of these new prospects is rated using the screening company's capacity and affinity ratings and is assigned to frontline fundraisers so that cultivation can begin. Each fundraiser receives a prospect's detail report printed directly from the screening information—no further information is deemed necessary to initiate contact.

EHN researchers begin the verification, rating, and assignment of the next tier of prospects: those with confirmed and unconfirmed assets of $1 million and above. As the researchers work through this next group, they prioritize and rate the prospects by wealth and affinity and assign each prospect to the appropriate frontline fundraiser.

As prospects near significant cultivation and eventual solicitation, more research will be done to update assets and discover further philanthropic giving, family foundations, company affiliations, and so on.

How to Keep Up with Online Resources

When you are first looking for prospect research resource vendors, you are likely to use a combination of free trials, recommendations from colleagues, and references like this book and its online counterpart, www.Research4Fundraisers.com. You can keep up with new tools by visiting exhibit halls at conferences, following the Association of Professional Researchers for Advancement (APRA) PRSPCT-L LISTSERV (www.aprahome.org), or finding a favorite research blog.

You might also consider using bookmarking software, such as Delicious.com, Digg.com, or one of the many others available. Keeping your favorite websites bookmarked with a description lets you keep track of great websites that you might not use often and reference them quickly when necessary.

If you pay to subscribe to a research tool, be sure to take advantage of any training offered. You might want to designate one person as the "power user" who can train other staff. Knowing how to use the tool effectively gives you a much better return on your investment.

SEARCH TECHNIQUES EVERY FUNDRAISER SHOULD KNOW

Whether you have prospect researchers on staff or you outsource your prospect research profiles to a consultant, every fundraiser should know some simple search techniques. Knowing how to find key pieces of information yourself allows you to explore new links to people early, giving you an advantage over those unable to operate online effectively. There will be times when your prospect is just so private that there is no information to be found in publicly held sources or when their stock holdings or corporate information is such that you will need an expert researcher to spend the time to unravel it, but don't let that keep you from getting your toes wet in the world of online research. In this section we will provide you with simple instructions and practical tips to help save you time and effort.

Step One: Find the Full Legal Name

Usually, we know our prospect's name and home address from given information, but there are times when the prospect is not using her full legal name or when we are researching someone new to us and do not have a home address. If we do not have the prospect's home address, we can often find at least the city and state from company biographies or news articles referencing the prospect. Now we know what county our prospect resides in.

In most cases, you should be able to locate your prospect's home at the city or county tax assessor's office. If you don't know the county, look up the town in a search engine, city-data.com, or use Wikipedia to find it.

When you find the real estate record, note how your prospect's name is listed. Also, if you find properties for which the mailing address is different from the property location, you may find that the mailing address is most likely the primary residence, or in some cases, the primary business address.

Beware: Very common names are difficult to research, especially if you do not start with a confirmed home address. Also, unless you purchase some kind of real estate search subscription, you will not know if your prospect owns property outside of his home county, such as a luxury condo in Aspen, Colorado, or a waterfront home in Miami Beach, Florida. See Table 3.1.

> Jim Williams, Vice President for Fund Development at Goodwill Industries–Suncoast, Inc. in Florida looks to see how long a prospect has owned his home. Planned givers often demonstrate consistent behavior, including owning the same home for many years.

Once you have confirmed ownership of the home address (and perhaps others), you will want to find the estimated market value of the property. Each county in each state across the country appraises and taxes real estate differently. To avoid confusion over appraised and assessed values from the municipality, consider the free resources listed in Table 3.2. As you explore them, you may find many other features that appeal to you beyond estimated property value.

| TABLE 3.1 | Real-Estate Ownership Sources |

Resource	Description
www.pulawski.net	This site lists every state and its counties and assessors. Not every county assessor has a searchable database, but most do or you can telephone them.
www.knowx.com	This will cost you money, but not much. Here you can search across the country for real estate under your prospect's name. And go ahead and get excited: the site allows you to search all kinds of other public records too.
Summary Look-Up Vendors	Many subscriptions have a real-estate search. Some of the most popular include Blackbaud's ResearchPoint, DonorSearch, LexisNexis for Development Professionals, and WealthEngine's FindWealth.

| TABLE 3.2 | Real-Estate Valuation Resources |

Resource	Description
www.trulia.com	Plug in an address and you will see a photo of the property from Google Street View and see an estimate of its value. Each listing has a description of the square footage and interior, and shows the last sale price and date.
www.zillow.com	Here you will get a "Z-estimate," a picture from Bing maps, and sometimes the year and sale price, which you will probably find in the tax assessor record too. Note that Zillow only covers residential property and not commercial property. Information on this site is also scarce in rural and some other areas.

Before you begin your search, take a moment and ask yourself, "who would be most likely to gather this information?" Salary information, for example, might be collected and published by a professional association. Information about leaders in a particular industry, like banking, may be covered by a specialty publication like *Banker & Tradesman*. A biography on a CEO would most likely be found at the company's website. Going directly to the likeliest source could save you valuable minutes of searching time.

Step Two: Become a Search-Engine Power User

Hopefully you now know your prospect's full legal name. Using a search engine next could very well be your final step, depending upon how deep you need to go. Using the search engine, you want to quickly find:

- Company or other biographical information, such as a LinkedIn.com profile: Many times you can find the prospect's current occupation, work history, education, nonprofit board directorships, and sometimes even spouse and children's names in the prospect's bio on a company website. In some cases this might just be enough to get you through your qualifying visit.
- News articles: Search results might provide full-text news articles or teasers for paid subscriptions. This alerts you that information is available. We cover how to get more of this information from a different source in Step Five further on.
- Public company insider: Search engine results are now finding Securities and Exchange Commission (SEC) documents on public company insiders. This alerts you that your prospect may be an insider. We cover public company insiders in more detail in Step Four below.
- Philanthropic interests: A high-profile philanthropist will quickly become evident from the search engine results. The prospect's favorite charitable organizations will post articles about gifts received and the prospect will likely appear in online donor

recognition reports. We cover searching for this information in more detail later in Step Three.

As you can see, if you only need some basic initial information about your prospect, a search engine can often reveal enough and provide good indicators that there could be much more information available about the individual in deeper web sources. For prospects with less information online or with very common names, good search technique becomes more important.

Table 3.3 gives you tips to help you become a power user of any search engine. Google is the most popular search engine, and its advanced search feature makes it easy to get the most out of it. As we have said before, good research technique takes practice.

Whatever search engine you use:

- If you get better at using it, you will find more information in less time.
- You will know which results are more likely to give you what you need and which ones will take you to a dead end.

Step Three: Find Giving History and Community Involvement

Giving History Online   Who cares how much wealth someone has if they won't give it away? Look for those gifts! You can search using Google's "search within a site or domain" feature described above or add keywords with your prospect's name such as *million, gift, director, trustee, donor, endow,* and so on. You can also use a paid subscription that specializes in providing philanthropic giving information.

If you are working within a very limited budget and can only purchase one subscription, consider a low-cost subscription to a service that provides philanthropic giving information, or try to be sure any other research subscription you buy includes a philanthropic giving database. After all, your best prospect is someone who makes gifts, not someone with great wealth who isn't philanthropic.

TABLE 3.3   **Search Engine Tips**

Tip	Description
Use quotes.	Putting quotations around a phrase or name finds the exact phrase, not just text containing all of those words. Try a search on each variation of your prospect's name. Here's an example of name variations. Try them one at a time: "jen filla" "jen j filla" "jennifer filla" "jennifer j filla" *Hot Tip*: Including a woman's maiden name sometimes brings up wedding announcements, obituaries, and other helpful info. Try: "jennifer ann smith jacoby" "jennifer smith jacoby"
Get better with keywords.	Especially if you need to narrow your search on a common name, try adding other keywords like the city or state (e.g., "tampa fl" or "ny"), company name, "Forbes" (you never know who might be listed in *Forbes*), and so on.
Use Google Advanced.	Use Google's advanced search feature! Click on the "Advanced Search" link, currently found at the bottom of the search results page. Especially helpful is the "search within a site or domain" part of the form. You can search a domain, such as every site that ends ".org" or ".edu," or search a website on which you know your prospect is likely to be mentioned, such as "Neumann.edu."
Use Google Verbatim.	Let's say you know your prospect's name and you do not want Google to find variations of this name which would provide unrelated hits for a famous person. You want the *exact* name. Run the same type of search as above, such as "frederic douglas," using quotes. Now look for "More Search Tools" in the left column of the page. Click on this option, look for "Verbatim," and click on this. Now Google finds the phrase "frederic douglas" *exactly*. That means the famous Frederick Douglass does not clutter your search results. To turn this feature off, look for the blue verbatim bar above your search results. Click the "x" at the far right to close it.
Still struggling?	Throw everything you know about the prospect into a search engine. Search for results using the prospect's e-mail, phone, or even physical address. Spell the prospect's name or company incorrectly; searching "Micheal Jordan" instead of "Michael Jordan," for example, turns up unexpected gold—including several official sites.

You may be wondering how giving-history search vendors are able to collect and sell gift information. Charitable donations are private and confidential, right? They are until the donor consents to the organization publicizing the gift information. Typically, a donor's giving history can be found in press releases and news articles, in donor recognition reports, or on the organization's or donor's websites. Donor recognition reports might be printed or online, or both.

Much as search engines send electronic harvesters out into the Internet to collect and index web pages so that we can search them, giving-history search vendors send electronic harvesters to collect information about gifts from online content, especially online donor recognition reports. The vendor will also supplement that data by scanning printed donor recognition reports into its database. See Table 3.4.

What is the key point here? If a gift is not published by the donor or organization, you will not find it—anywhere. Giving-history search vendors do not have special passwords to private information. They can only produce gift information that has been released into the public domain. Also consider that your prospect could be highly philanthropic but give anonymously.

Nonprofit Directors and Foundation Directors   Now that you are a search-engine power searcher, you may have found references to your prospect being a nonprofit or foundation director. These are strong indicators of philanthropic inclination! Finding this information from

TABLE 3.4   **Giving Search Subscriptions**

Vendor	Description
www.nozasearch.com	This is a Blackbaud product that allows you to search by name and other variables to find giving history.
www.donorsearch.net; www.iwave.com; www.wealthengine.com	These companies all offer products that bundle various search capabilities, one of which is giving-history searches. Just as there are many search engines besides Google, each of these giving-history search vendors will yield slightly different results.

search engines can seem serendipitous, and you might be wondering if there are search vendors dedicated to this pursuit, just as there are for giving-history searches.

> If you find that your prospect has established a trust or is a trustee of a family foundation, the IRS Form 990-PF will tell you whether she or other family members have made contributions. Look on the first page of the IRS Form 990-PF to see if there have been contributions. Near the end of the tax return will be a description of who made the contribution and how much each individual gave. This can help you in determining their major gift capacity.

There are vendors, but don't underestimate what you can find yourself using search engines. The higher a person's passion for a cause, the more likely he is to talk about his volunteer activities, including serving on an organization's board of directors, and the more likely you are to find that information through your searches.

The most popular vendors that can help you find nonprofit and foundation directorships were not necessarily created with that purpose in mind. People usually either want to find foundations to fund their programs, or they want to find nonprofit organizations they can give money to or become involved with somehow. The information they collect for those purposes serves us well as we search for individual directorships or perhaps even nonprofit employee compensation. See Table 3.5.

Political Contributions   Federal election campaign contributions are regulated by the Federal Election Commission (FEC). Federal, state, and local political giving can usually be searched online for free. Information about political giving is helpful for the following reasons:

- When a contribution is made, donors are asked for their city, state, and zip code, as well as their employer.

TABLE 3.5	Foundation and Nonprofit Directorship Vendors

Vendor	Description
http://foundationcenter.org	This not-for-profit company offers a free search by foundation name. Beware: The search is exact, so use as little of the name as possible. The company also offers a subscription service, which allows searches by name for trustees, officers, and donors.
www.foundationsearch.com	This company has no free searches, but like the Foundation Center Online, its features include search by name functionality.
www.guidestar.org	Guidestar includes many foundations in its database and is the most robust subscription available for operating nonprofit organizations like your own. This not-for-profit company has some free searches, but its subscription service is what allows you to search by name for nonprofit directors.

- Political giving is a form of community participation and, especially when no other forms of giving are found, suggests some level of inclination to give as well as their level of disposable income.

See Table 3.6.

Step Four: Find Occupational Information

Private Companies   Hopefully you have found some great information about your prospect already using a search engine. Keep in mind that if your prospect owns a private company, information about revenues or profits is self-reported or estimated. There is no requirement for disclosure. Many times news articles, social media, and the company's website provide the best information, but don't neglect your local library. The reference librarian or business section librarian may be especially helpful in your search for information on a local privately held company, and many libraries have a range of online databases you can search for free with your library card. See Table 3.7.

TABLE 3.6 **Political Contributions**

Source	Description
http://cqmoneyline.com	For better federal giving results, we recommend that you click on the "Advanced Donor Search" link just below the search box on the home page. After your results have loaded, look to the right of the search fields at the top of the page to find the "Excel download" link.
www.opensecrets.org	This site lets you search for federal giving and also for soft money contributions. It does not offer the option to download search results.
www.followthemoney.org	Search this site for state giving. We recommend using the "Advanced Search" option for better results.

TABLE 3.7 **Private Companies**

Source	Description
www.manta.com	Go through the free registration. Then search for the company name. Manta gives you estimated annual revenues from a mix of sources as well as other info for free.
www.aspireresearchgroup .com/corpname.html	This is a collection of the state web pages that offer incorporation-record searches or the place to call for them.
www.inc.com/magazine/ 20101101/the-2010-business-valuation-guide.html	If you are feeling ambitious, you can read about valuing a private business from *Inc.* magazine.

Private companies are used in many ways. Your prospect's primary company may be operating a business, such as selling widgets, but you may find that she is an officer of private companies that do not appear to have any business purpose. This is most often the case with entrepreneurs. Keep in mind that people with significant wealth may be using a company to hold and manage their assets. One prospect set up a family limited partnership—for example, Clark and Vivien Gable Ltd.—every time he sold a successful company he had founded. He used these companies to hold the proceeds of the sale. Through these limited partnerships he invested in other private companies and made other high-risk investments.

Public Company Insiders   If you know that your prospect is a top executive or a director of a public company, you can find detailed information about compensation and stockholdings. It is not the easiest reading and when it is really important, such as when you are nearing a solicitation, this might be a very good time to look for an expert prospect researcher to provide you with a profile. See Table 3.8.

TABLE 3.8   **Public Companies**

Source	Description
www.j3sg.com	This company offers a free search by insider name and the results are easy to read.
www.sec.gov; www.secinfo.com	The SEC is the primary source, but the filings can be a tough read. At SEC.gov, search by company name or by name under the "full text past 4 years" option. SECinfo.com has easier search functions, but you still have to read the filings to get answers.
www.marketwatch.com; www.yahoofinance.com	Find the company's ticker symbol from its website or a search-engine search and put it into the search box. These sites do a great job of organizing information and have insider lists.

Three of the most common instances when your prospect's stock-holding in a publicly traded company is made public are when:

1. The prospect is a top executive.
2. The prospect is a director.
3. The prospect owns 10 percent or more of the company's stock.

There are some other times when stock ownership is made public, but they are much less common.

Step Five: Find General and Biographical Information

Hopefully a quick search-engine search for your prospect's name gives you a great bio and a real estate search tells you that his or her humble abode is worth millions, but if not, consider a few more sources. See Table 3.9.

TABLE 3.9	General and Biographical

Source	Description
www.pipl.com	Please do *not* assume everything found here is perfectly matched to your prospect, but if your search-engine search left you dissatisfied, you might find leads using this site.
www.zoominfo.com	Partly free, ZoomInfo keeps its own copies of information found on the Internet. That means that even though the original web page has disappeared, you may be able to find a copy here.
Your public library	As mentioned earlier, your public or university library has incredible sources available to you for free with your library card. Most libraries have online news and business databases and much more. If you are not sure, call a reference librarian.

As you begin using search engines to find biographical information, you will notice all kinds of companies promising to find everything there is to know about your prospect—for a fee. Be careful. Frequently, these online services are unreliable or violate ethics rules. Matching information to your prospect accurately requires careful attention, something electronic software struggles to do well.

Two of the best sources of biographical information are obituaries and marriage announcements. These two resources often provide history and family connections and can be found by searching online news databases, funeral home websites, and search engines. If you are researching a woman, try using her first, maiden, and surname in quotes (e.g., "Vivien Leigh Gable") to get better results.

Other Search Concepts

Less Is Often Much More   In a search, *less* is almost always going to give you *more* information. Most of us follow this rule unknowingly by typing in our search terms without quotes. Quotes limit our search results to those that match our terms in the exact order. In a search, it may be best to start without limiting your results.

Here are some examples of when less is more:

- Use a prospect's last name only and then add a first name and other terms as needed.
- Start with a state and add the city and finally the street or company name if needed.
- Use the most identifiable word or words in a company name and narrow down the search later with the exact name.

The exception: If you have a common name or a *very* common name, the game changes and you have to adjust your tactics, or less will become way-too-much more.

Savvy Conversational Technique   Sometimes it is the frontline fundraiser who sources the most important information directly from the prospect through conversation. Before making a substantial contact with a prospect, decide ahead of time what you want to accomplish. Do you want to qualify the person for capacity or interest? Come up with some conversation topics that will help you, and then share the information you have found with your prospect researcher or research consultant, if you decide to request further information.

Some topics you might talk to your prospect about:

- Family:
  - Who are these handsome children in the photo?
  - Where did you meet your husband/wife?
- Vacations:
  - That's a great sunset picture! Were you on vacation?
- Volunteer activities and why they give:
  - What do you like most about volunteering at our organization?
  - Have you ever been disappointed in a gift?
  - How do you decide to make a gift?
- Occupation/business:
  - What made you choose engineering?
  - How did your business get started?
- Collections:
  - These figurines are beautiful! How long have you been collecting?

Asking questions that help you discover a prospect's passions and give insight into her interests and needs is critical prospect research that is best done in person whenever possible. We all know there are a lot of wealthy people in the world who do not make gifts. If there is no passion for the mission, the likelihood of a major gift becomes small.

Being able to navigate to and through the first visit with a prospect is a critical prospect research skill for every frontline fundraiser. Hale T. Peffal Jr., Director of Development at The Center for Autism in Pennsylvania, offers the following tips:

- *Meet in person:* Don't be shy about asking to meet the fascinating person who just made a wonderful first gift to you!
- *Let them choose the place:* The prospect will choose a place where he is most comfortable, and that is good for building rapport.
- *Make good conversation:* Be aware of everything about the prospect and use it to make conversation. Mention these things in your thank-you note.
- *End with an invitation to the next step:* Make the first meeting in person at a place of comfort, but the second meeting could be a tour of your organization. Don't end without a next step that continues the conversation!

CAPACITY RATINGS: PUTTING THE INFORMATION TOGETHER

After you have gathered key information about the assets and overall wealth of your prospect, you may want to determine a capacity rating. As we will discuss in Chapter 4, Donor Relationship Management, capacity ratings are a key piece in your prospect tracking system. Together with other ratings, capacity ratings help you prioritize your prospect list so that you spend the most resources on the individuals most likely and able to make a gift.

There are various ways to define a capacity rating from individual donor research. For the purposes of this book, capacity rating:

- Is a major-gift dollar range for a gift over five years if only one gift was made.

- Is strictly based on wealth indicators and not on affinity or inclination.
- Suggests ability to give without considering unknown liabilities.
- Is *not* a solicitation amount.

Once you have gathered some initial information about a prospect, you may be hoping for a precise scientific method for determining your prospect's ability to make a gift. As of the time of publication of this book, there is no such thing. What we do have are indicators of philanthropic trends among wealthy individuals derived from sources such as census data, IRS tax return data on the wealthy, and other research studies on this group of individuals.

Using these information sources, prospect researchers have developed many different formulas and methods for estimating capacity. Single-asset formulas are the most general and also the easiest to use. Single-asset formulas can be used in combination to help give you a better idea of a person's capacity, but they are likely to provide you with conflicting results. The more data you have, the more robust and less subjective your capacity rating will be.

Following are some common single-asset formulas you can use to help determine capacity:

- *Real-estate value*: Dollar amount (> $400,000) × 5 years × (4% or 3%)
- *Salary*: Salary × (5% or 10%) × 5 years
- *Political contributions*: Dollar amount in one cycle × 20
- *Annual giving*: Dollar amount in one year × 20
- *Direct stock holdings*: Direct stock holdings × 5% or (Direct stock holdings ÷ .20) × 5%

For example, let's say that you find your prospect, Dr. Jacoby:

- Owns her home in New York City with a value of $1.5 million.
- Is a cardiac surgeon, which according to the AMGA Medical Group Compensation and Financial Survey provides a median annual salary of $533,000. Her known annual giving in the last year was a cumulative amount of $5,000.

Her single-asset formulas would reveal gift capacity as follows:

- $1,500,000 × 5 years × .04 = $300,000
- $533,000 × 5 years × .05 = $133,250
- $5,000 × 20 = $100,000

You might decide that her capacity could reasonably be $100,000 to $300,000. However, you might also know that she received a substantial inheritance from her parents based on news articles or that she made a $1 million pledge to her alma mater last month.

While we can't truly know a prospect's capacity, we can reasonably assign a capacity rating that helps us prioritize our prospect pool to ensure that we spend the most time with the prospects that are likely to provide the most benefit to our organization and the mission it serves. Remember, this is not the ask amount. The ask amount incorporates capacity plus passion and closeness to the organization.

When talking about an individual's capacity or wealth, it is tempting to use the term "net worth." According to Investopedia,[1] net worth is "the amount by which assets exceed liabilities." Since we use only publicly available sources, we cannot know with certainty a person's complete assets. For example, a person may have an extensive stock portfolio and yet, if he is not an insider as defined by the SEC, none of that information is public.

Even more so, we cannot know a person's liabilities. Because of this, it is not possible for us to know our prospect's net worth. There are some capacity formulas that attempt to guess a person's net worth based on known assets and affluent research study findings,[2] but they are only guesses.

---

[1]"Net worth," *Investopeida*, www.investopedia.com/terms/n/networth.asp#axzz1 hr1bZ1Pl.
[2]"Sneak Peek at the Upcoming Ipsos Mendelsohn Affluent Survey," *Luxury Insights* (blog), August 11, 2010, http://blog.luxuryhomemarketing.com/2010/08/ipsos.html.

Summary

As you begin looking for information on prospective donors, first consider establishing levels of research based on where the prospect stands in
the gift cycle. Do you need to confirm philanthropic inclination, wealth
capacity and connection to your organization for someone you have
just identified or do you need to know everything possible to strategize
for your solicitation? Establishing different levels of research helps you
use time and resources efficiently. Creating profile levels around the gift
cycle is one option, such as the following:

- Identification/qualification profile.
- Cultivation profile.
- Solicitation profile.

Prospect profiles of individuals have five main areas of information as
follows:

1. Biographical information.
2. Relationship to your organization.
3. Community involvement and giving.
4. Occupation/career history.
5. Assets.

Prospect profiles of companies have four main areas of information:

1. Contact information.
2. Company description.
3. Company philanthropy.
4. Relationship to your organization.

Prospect profiles of foundations also have four main areas of information:

1. Contact information.
2. Areas of interest and limitations.
3. Recent philanthropic giving.
4. Relationship to your organization.

As you look for tools and resources your office can use to find information on individual, company and foundation donors, consider how many profiles you might need in any given year based on the number of major gift solicitations you expect to make.

Even if you are not doing the research on prospects yourself, there are some search techniques you should know to quickly find the information you want. Consider becoming a power user of your favorite search engine, subscription, or other online tool. Becoming very well versed even in one or just a few tools will serve you better than knowing only a little bit about many different tools. If you work in a large development office with a prospect research department, this will help you be self-sufficient and allow the research team to do more strategic work.

The advent of online searching has changed the way we fundraise, but some core human principles still apply. Do not overlook the importance of talking directly with your prospects and talking with their peers. These sources still yield some of the most important information you could ever know about your prospect and are incredibly useful in helping you find more. Be smart about your searching, and take a moment before you begin to map out the most direct route to the information you are looking for.

There are some standard, one-value formulas in the prospect research field that can help you get a feel for your prospect's capacity. While these formulas help put the information you know about a prospect into perspective, there is often much more we do not know about a prospect that could have an impact on his capacity. Give careful thought to the wealth found, giving history, and all the other factors you know about a prospect before assigning a capacity rating.

FOR FURTHER READING

Hancks, Meredith. *Getting Started in Prospect Research: What You Need to Know to Find Who You Need to Find*. Rancho Santa Margarita, CA: CharityChannel, 2011.

Hart, Ted, James M. Greenfield, Pamela M. Gignac, and Christopher Carnie. *Major Donors: Finding Big Gifts in Your Database and Online.* Hoboken, NJ: John Wiley & Sons, 2006.

Hogan, Cecilia. *Prospect Research: A Primer for Growing Nonprofits.* Boston: Jones and Bartlett, 2004 (revised 2007).

Sherman, Chris, and Gary Price. *The Invisible Web: Uncovering Information Sources Search Engines Can't See.* Medford, NJ: CyberAge, 2001.

Sobel, Andrew, and Jerold Panas. *Power Questions: Build Relationships, Win New Business, and Influence Others.* Hoboken, NJ: Wiley, 2012.

CHAPTER 4

Donor Relationship Management

A relationship management system is like a household budget. You can do without it, but when money matters, you will find yourself coming up short.

Identifying prospects is a time-consuming and costly task. Once you have a group of prospects, you will need a system to engage and move them toward a significant gift. If you are a small office, you might start with a simple system that tracks only a few items. If you are a large office, you might need more complexity and staff dedicated to managing the process.

The last thing you want to do is wander aimlessly after your prospects for years. Don't hope that they will make a gift. Provide the kind of attention and respect that will effectively and efficiently lead them to make a substantial investment in your cause. Using a relationship management system gives you the framework to make steady forward progress.

This chapter walks you through the three main pieces of a relationship management system and what those pieces might look like for you. We explain how you can create your own system and provide you with sample reports so you have a clear idea of how it works.

TABLE 4.1   **Prospecting versus Dating**

Relationship Stage	Prospecting	Dating
Identification/ Qualification	You are introduced by a board member to someone who has all the right wealth and philanthropy indicators to be a major-gift prospect for your organization. The prospect wants to visit your organization to learn more and you promise to call. Two weeks later you finally call and your prospect is a little standoffish, but agrees to visit.	Your brother introduces you to a person to whom you are very attracted. S/he gives you a phone number and encourages you to call. Two weeks later you finally call and s/he almost doesn't remember you, but agrees to go on a date.
Cultivation	The prospect is so excited by the visit s/he sends you an e-mail the minute s/he gets back to the office. You don't think about the prospect again until three months later when you are planning an event and want to invite the prospect, but you never wrote anything down about your meeting and forget why the prospect was so excited when s/he visited.	Your date goes really well. You have a lot of interests in common and are both pretty excited. Your date texts you that night to let you know how much s/he enjoyed it. A few weeks go by and you decide to call for another date. You remember she said something about vacation plans, but you can't remember what. You call and s/he is in Aruba. S/he laughs that you are so absentminded.
Solicitation	Two years go by with sporadic contact. Now you are gearing up for a campaign and wonder if the prospect would be a good lead donor. You schedule a visit at the prospect's home to discuss the campaign planning, but s/he isn't very enthused.	Two years go by like this and s/he knows all about you, but you still can't remember how many siblings s/he has or what the pet's name is. You take your date to a romantic restaurant and casually mention friends who are getting married. You ask if s/he ever thinks about marriage. S/he chokes on the appetizer before answering.

WHAT IS A RELATIONSHIP MANAGEMENT SYSTEM?

A relationship management system is a collection of information and tasks that tracks and directs the actions required to convert a prospect into a major gift donor. You might hear other people refer to it as moves management, prospect management, or, in the business world, customer relationship management (CRM). We are all talking about the same thing. Consider the scenarios in Table 4.1 to start thinking about how a system might improve your major gift program performance.

Unlike most dating scenarios, you will likely need to keep track of anywhere from 10 to 200 people. That is a lot of dates! At any one time you should have a group of prospects that you actively and frequently contact. Sporadic, generic calls and visits do not lead to close and productive relationships. Parting with a large sum of one's hard-earned money is a personal decision that often anticipates a long-term relationship with your organization.

Now imagine that every day you arrive in the office, check your e-mail, and then check your "relationship to-do list," which we are going to call an action report. This everyday activity ensures you are spending the right amount of energy on the right prospects. If it takes as much energy to close on a $100,000 gift as it does a $1 million gift, a clear and disciplined focus is required to maximize your time so that you can close on more gifts and larger gifts.

The most successful frontline fundraisers I have known share several characteristics: They are excellent listeners, they take time to understand donor perspectives and motivations, they engage many people in building each relationship (rather than viewing prospects as "theirs"), and they inspire belief and confidence in everyone with whom they work. They understand that all wealthy people are not necessarily philanthropic, and they remain focused on those that are.

They also record and share information, recognizing that an organization's best prospective donor is their last donor.

—RONALD J. SCHILLER, Senior Vice President for Business Development, Lois L. Lindauer Searches

Every time you complete a task on your action report, such as scheduling or attending a meeting with a prospect, you record what happened and then create a new, dated action item for that prospect. Periodically, you run a report on all of your prospects to ensure:

- That you are moving your prospects through cultivation toward a gift in a timely way.
- That you are spending the most time with the prospects who have the most wealth and passion for your organization.

If you are a solo development officer or working in a small office, do not be intimidated! You can create and maintain a relationship management system that will give you the framework for achieving major gift success. Choose the fundamental items you want to track, select your best prospects, and get moving.

In a small shop, persistence and sincerity in your actions is key. Keep your system simple and actionable.

There will be times when work is overwhelming and it is difficult to keep an action report updated. There will also be times when you forget to record your notes about a meeting with your prospect. But staying on top of these tasks to the degree that you can will help you be more efficient and raise more money in the long run.

Your relationship management system needs to keep track of more than just your direct contacts with your prospects. You also want to know things like:

- How close is the prospect to us?
- Is the prospect philanthropic?

- What is the prospect's capacity to make a major gift?
- What are the prospect's philanthropic objectives and which align with our needs?
- What size gift do we think the prospect will give to us?
- Is the prospect ready to give?
- Who else can and should be involved in building the prospect's relationship with us?

If you already have a relationship management system in place, you know this, but if you are planning to create a system, keep in mind that a relationship management system will add tasks to your workload. The power of a relationship management system is its ability to focus and channel your major gifts efforts.

Ideally, when you create a relationship management process that systematically tracks information in your database and manages the human element, you can move from identification to solicitation faster and at higher gift levels—in other words, you raise more money. You also gain in a number of ways:

- You stay *focused* on those donor prospects most likely to move your mission forward through engagement and giving.
- Through internal review meetings, you *work as a team* to craft cultivation and solicitation strategies.
- By articulating your cultivation and solicitation strategies you become *more efficient*, moving prospects more quickly in the direction they want to go.
- With well-planned reports you can chart your progress toward your fundraising goals and clearly *see what you need to do* to move forward with your prospect pool.

THE THREE MOVING PIECES

Your relationship management system has three big moving pieces. Each of these pieces moves the others, creating the momentum you need to grow your major gifts program. See Figure 4.1.

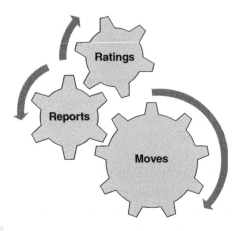

FIGURE 4.1   **Three Pieces of Relationship Management**

1. *Rating your best prospects*: Prioritizing your prospects keeps you focused on the best ones.
2. *Moving your prospects*: You are moving prospects through the gift cycle. This includes (a) actions like phone calls and meetings that happen on the calendar, and (b) recording the results of those actions. These actions should be qualifying, cultivating, soliciting, and stewarding your donors and prospects.
3. *Reporting on your prospects*: Human nature has us contacting the people we like most, and they are not always our best prospects. The most effective fundraisers measure their success through regular reporting.

Rating Your Best Prospects

The very best prospects in your pool are those who have:

- *Affinity:* The closeness the prospect feels to your organization.
- *Capacity:* The level of wealth or ability to make a major gift.

- *Inclination or propensity to give:* A history of making gifts to your organization and to other nonprofits.

(You may hear other fundraisers refer to these characteristics as *linkage, ability,* and *inclination.*)

You might want to take exception to this for planned-giving prospects. The most reliable indicator for planned-giving prospects in your database is usually affinity. It is a better indicator than wealth!

How a prospect is connected to your organization is critical information necessary for cultivation, but it is not a primary indicator of capacity or inclination. It is important to spend your resources on those prospects most capable and inclined.

You will want to discover how the prospect is linked or connected to your organization, if this is not already evident, after the prospect has been highly rated. This is often uncovered in the initial research that is done or by the frontline fundraiser during discovery and cultivation. Linkage or connection is not typically a piece of information stored separately in the database, but it could be easily stored in a text field if you wanted to retrieve and review it in the future.

Moving Your Prospects

In order to effectively move your prospects toward a gift and steward those who make gifts, you need to keep track of:

- *Actions:* These are the substantial contacts you have with your prospects that deepen their engagement with your organization and move them closer to a major gift.
- *Major gift proposals:* Knowing what gift proposals you have submitted and closed lets you evaluate your performance and ensure you actually close on the gift. This could be included as part of your actions.
- *Readiness:* Is this person newly identified, being cultivated, ready to solicit, or in stewardship? Did they decline a recent solicitation?

Do you know why? Tracking this information helps you manage your time to ensure you don't miss a gift opportunity.

- *Target gift amount:* Notice that this is different from the capacity range. The target gift amount is what you think the prospect will actually give your organization, and considers capacity, affinity, and other things you learn about the prospect that impact their ability to give.
- *Target gift date:* Selecting a reasonable target gift date keeps you feeling the urgency of your actions. If the target gift date is not met, you will need to answer why not.

In addition, if you are a manager, are tasked with cultivating a large prospect pool, or need to coordinate multiple solicitors, you may also want to keep track of:

- *Cultivation strategy:* This is your big picture road map for the direction you need to travel to bring the prospect closer to the organization. As this strategy develops, it incorporates the prospect's interests, influencers, and other characteristics that help you make the right ask at the right time to the right person.
- *Assigned prospect manager:* Someone has to be accountable for leading the prospect to a gift. You might find yourself assigning different types of managers to the prospect, such as a staff manager, a leadership manager, or a volunteer manager, but there should be one person who has overall responsibility for each prospect.
- *Prospect type:* This can be helpful when you have multiple major-gift initiatives or want to track different levels or types of prospects. For example, your organization may be pursuing endowed scholarships, capital gifts, or other special projects. You may be tracking individual, corporate, and foundation prospects. You might also use this field if you want to be sure the same donor is not asked for an annual gift, a major gift, and a planned gift at the same time!

Reporting on Your Progress

We know that successful fundraising programs measure performance. Without measurements, we end the fiscal year wondering why we did not reach our fundraising goals.

Sometimes people confuse a relationship management system with a software program of some kind. We use software to help us, but a relationship management system includes the very human actions of visiting and asking our prospects for gifts.

Creating a relationship management system for your organization should include regular reporting. Recording prospect ratings and actions in your donor database often makes reporting an automated process. But even if you are a solo fundraiser and are not using your database for this purpose, you still need to record your prospect information in a way that can be reported.

As we discuss storing the tracking data, and as you begin crafting a system for your organization, always think ahead to how you will report on the information you are tracking.

If you find that you are collecting and entering a particular type of information into your database that is never pulled into a report, you might want to stop tracking that information.

CREATING YOUR OWN SYSTEM

Carefully planning now where to store information will save time, resources, and money later. It is a best practice to store all information that you will want to retrieve later in your donor database. However, if you are a solo practitioner you might find yourself using a combination of database, calendar, word processing, and spreadsheet software applications to keep you on track.

If you decide to record relationship management information in your database and you do not have a deep set of skills in that area, consider consulting your database vendor for advice or hiring an assistant or a consultant. Common mistakes configuring fields in the database include the following:

- Creating a field that cannot be retrieved through a standard report.
- Creating a field with the wrong format, such as using a text field when you want to be able to query on dates.
- Using a text field where users type their information and being unable to query on the field later for reporting.

CASE STUDY

Ed, a database manager, put the final touches on the field configuration in the donor database for a new relationship management system. He made a presentation to the development team and everyone was ready to begin recording information. The vice president just wanted one last change. She thought that, given the pending campaign, there should be another level of capacity ratings at $5 million+. Ed said that would be an easy change to make and the meeting ended.

When Ed went back to his desk and began to make the change he realized he would have to re-enter the entire table he had created for that field. Here is what the original table looked like:

1. $1 million+
2. $500,000–$999,999
3. $100,000–$499,999
4. $50,000–$99,999
5. $1,000–$49,999

Ed was very relieved that he had caught his mistake before the system was in use. He reversed the number order of the capacity ratings so that he could easily add ratings at the top in the future. His table now looked like this:

6. $5 million+
5. $1 million–$4,999,999
4. $500,000–$999,999
3. $100,000–$499,999
2. $50,000–$99,999
1. $1,000–$49,999

Tips on Entering Relationship Management Information

Regardless of what kind of software you are using, we all know what a headache it is to enter data over time only to find that we can't pull it back out reliably because of things like inconsistent terms and codes, duplicate records, data entry errors, people not marked as deceased, and other problems. Here are a few general data maintenance tips regarding relationship management:

- *Use drop-down fields:* Try to find a way to store the information that requires the entry to be chosen from a predefined list. This makes it easy to pull reports.
- *Keep fields close:* If you can, keep the fields you are using for relationship management information close together, such as all on one tab or data-entry page. This makes it easy to see what you need to be entering—and usually makes it easier to find it if you create a custom report.
- *Be consistent:* If you are using a drop-down field, this is less of an issue, but if you are writing the subject line in your action report, consistency can make the difference between a one-click report and a digging expedition. Keep in mind what you will want to know later. Here are some questions to think about:
  - Is my performance measured by the number of actions or do I need to know which actions were discovery visits versus general cultivation?
  - Is there a drop-down field to label the action a discovery visit or can I preface the subject line with the words "discovery visit"?
    Some types of database software make recording and reporting easier than others.

If you find yourself using a calendar and spreadsheet combination to track actions, consistency can save you a lot of time. Consider labeling all your major gift calls and visits the same way. If you do, you

(Continued)

can search using those keywords to get a list. Something like "MG Call-Tertius Lydgate" (where MG is major gift) or "MG Visit-Joanna Jones" is short but effective. Now you could search for every instance of "MG Call" in your calendar, or search for "Tertius Lydgate" if you forget when you last contacted him.

Creating Prospect Ratings

Prospect ratings are a key part of a relationship management system. We are all familiar with how important our personal credit ratings are when we apply for a new credit card or shop for a loan. Prospect ratings perform the same function in the fundraising office. Prospect ratings allow fundraisers to sort their prospects so they can stay focused on the best ones.

Multiple Prospect Ratings   Table 4.2 demonstrates a prospect rating system using multiple fields. Why use this kind of system? Using separate, multiple ratings allows you to use the information for many different purposes. In addition to major gifts, you might use these ratings to help pull your gala invitation list or help segment an annual appeal. Keeping capacity separate from affinity and inclination can also help you pull better planned-giving lists. Especially if you do not have much more than giving recorded in your database, affinity can be a better indicator than wealth for planned-giving prospects.

Keeping capacity ratings and target ask amounts the same as your organization's donor recognition levels or campaign gift levels helps everyone—donors, prospects, staff and leadership—stay focused on the priorities and makes life easier at end-of-year reporting time.

TABLE 4.2

Multiple Prospect Ratings

Rating Type	What Is It?	Where Does It Come from?	What It Might Look Like
Affinity (also *Linkage*)	A measure of how close the prospect is to your organization.	The prospect's link to your organization, such as *advocate, event attendee, service recipient, volunteer,* or *staff member*; or a determination based on donor contact.	*Insider, Active, Inactive, Distant, Uninterested.*
Capacity (also *Ability*)	A measure of the largest donation that a prospect could give, a transformational gift, or the calculation of what a prospect could give to only one organization for a five-year period.	Various metrics could be used, including: 2 to 5 percent of a prospect's total visible assets; highest past gift; a peer review; or a fundraising professional's best judgment.	A numeric value: 25,000; 50,000; etc. *or* a range like 10,000 to 49,999, 50,000 to 99,999 etc. *or* an alphabetic value: *A, B, C, D,* etc. could correspond to different gift levels.
Inclination	A measure of an individual's demonstrated overall philanthropy.	Evidence of past donations to you or another organization.	*Donor to us, Donor to us and others, Donor to others, Non-donor.*
Readiness or Prospect Stage (Small Office)	Which stage of the gift cycle the prospect is in.	A determination by the fundraiser assigned to the prospect.	*Identified, Qualified, Disqualified, Cultivation, Solicitation, Stewardship.*
Readiness (Large Office)	The likelihood that a donor will respond positively to a request for a major gift.	Determined by the fundraiser assigned to the prospect or other insider knowledge.	A numeric value: *1 = Ready to be solicited, 2 = Ask within the next six months, 3 = Ask within the next 12 to 18 months, 4 = Ask pending, 5 = Ask successful, 6 = Ask refused.*
Target Ask	While a donor's capacity rating might be $1 million, the Target Ask considers other factors such as readiness, type of gift, and family or other issues impacting ability to give.	Based on the strategy set for the donor.	Usually, the actual amount that will be asked of the prospect in an upcoming solicitation.

Numerical Prospect Ratings Christopher Carnie, co-founder of Factary in the UK, created a practical prospect rating system that drops inclination and combines affinity, capacity, and readiness to create a numerical rating. See the example with instructions in Table 4.3.

Why would you use a numerical rating like this? This numerical rating quickly prioritizes your list of prospects into distinct groups. If you are a start-up, a one-person shop, or working at an organization with just a few prospects, this is a quick system to get you focused fast. You could enter the final rating on the prospect's record in your donor database or keep it in a separate spreadsheet.

Alphabetical Prospect Ratings Maybe it is the influence of those childhood school report cards, but many people relate to ratings based on the alphabet. The alphabetical prospect rating system illustrated in Figure 4.2 is loosely based on the Boston Consulting Group matrix developed for businesses in the early 1970s.[1] The fundraising model places an emphasis on affinity. This is why it is often used in campaigns and major-gift programs where prospects must feel very close to the organization before trusting it with a large or transformational gift.

TABLE 4.3   **Numerical Prospect Ratings**

Name	Capacity	Affinity	Readiness	Multiplied Rating
Ron	3	3	2	18
Susan	2	3	1	6
Chris	1	3	3	9
Telia	2	2	2	8
Leslie	3	3	3	27

Instructions: On a scale of one to three (where three is the highest), rate each of your prospects based on their capacity to make a major gift, the closeness of their relationship to you ("affinity"), and their readiness to be asked based on where they are in cultivation. Multiply each of the numbers on an individual's line to find their score. (Multiplying rather than adding creates more distinct groups of prospects.)

[1] For a description of the Boston Consulting Group model, visit www.quick mba.com/strategy/matrix/bcg.

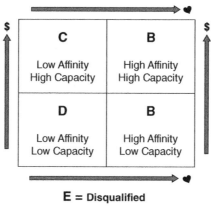

FIGURE 4.2   **Alphabetical Prospect Ratings**

Vendor Ratings   Most vendors that provide data-mining and wealth-screening services now also provide some type of ratings for the prospects identified. Some vendors allow you to tweak the ratings system yourself to weight it towards the information that you find most useful (multiple properties or stock holdings for planned-giving prospecting, for example).

Be sure to find out from your vendor what factors they use to create their ratings so that you can make a good decision about whether to import those ratings into your database.

You should be aware that all information you upload can become dated—and for that reason, if possible, you want to be sure to attach a date stamp to any vendor ratings.

Recording Prospect Moves

Once your prospects are rated, you have a prioritized list of people to contact, engage, and solicit for gifts. Connecting with prospects is where most frontline fundraisers shine. This is where you discover who and what inspires your prospect and how to translate that into a substantial gift for your organization.

How to Record Actions   Regardless of how good your memory is, it is still fallible. Only so many people and their personal details can be remembered. That's why it's so important to record visit information right away in a contact report and record cultivation plans and actions in your database as you make decisions. Recording your contact notes and strategies will help you achieve the next highest level of success in major gifts.

Remember, you are building a relationship between the organization and the prospect that should continue long after you leave your employment. We know it takes as much effort to secure a $100,000 gift as it does a $1 million gift, but if the $100,000 donor is a really nice person you can relate to and the $1 million donor is not . . . human nature pulls us toward the more likable prospect.

Prospect ratings keep us honest about who our best prospects are, and actions show clearly how well we have cultivated those prospects. If you truly want to raise the most money you can for your organization and the mission it serves, recording your actions, most especially face-to-face visits, will help get you there. By recording your actions you can measure things like:

- How many contacts did it take to reach a gift?
- How many prospects did it take to get one gift?
- What was the average number of months to reach the gift?
- What does a successful cultivation look like? An unsuccessful one?

Whether your donor database has a place to record dated actions, or whether you used a calendar/word processing combination, there are two major criteria to live by:

1. *If it is not in the system, it did not happen.* Summarize conversations with the prospect and document only what is needed to further the donor relationship. If you would be embarrassed to have a prospect read something in your action report, do not include it.
2. *There should always be a future action.* Even after you secure the gift, you should continue to contact the donor as part of good stewardship.

If you are in a large office, action reports are likely a part of your performance evaluation. You are rewarded for properly recording the information. But if you are in a smaller office or it is not part of your performance goals, you should still follow Nike's tagline and *just do it*. No excuses. No complaints about time. Immediately record your actions and update the record as needed. It takes less effort than you think and the rewards are larger gifts.

Lisa Howley, Director of Relationship Management at the Johns Hopkins Institutions, uses a clear definition of an action you may wish to adopt at your organization. An action must meet at least one of the following criteria:

- Outcomes met the purpose of the contact.
- Contact advanced the prospect relationship.
- Something new was learned.
- Contact resulted in a next step.

Recording your actions is important, but not as important as the actions themselves. Fundraisers need to find the balance between the key pieces of information to record and what can be omitted. If you find that your action list is becoming burdensome or overwhelming, reevaluate what you are recording.

For example, if you need to schedule a visit, create an open action and keep it open until the visit is scheduled, moving the date forward each time you leave a message or send an e-mail. Using an action this way keeps you looking to your system for all actions you need to accomplish. But do you need to carefully paste each e-mail exchange or record each word from a message? Very likely not. The goal is to schedule the visit, and the conversations necessary to schedule the appointment probably don't contain new or valuable information.

Solicitation Proposals   Regardless of the size and complexity of your organization or the donor database software you are using, you will want to keep track of your major-gift proposals. At the very least you need to know what proposals are outstanding so that you can be sure to close them in a timely way. If there is a preconfigured spot in your donor database for proposals, you might find that there are standard reports associated with proposals that will not require customization.

Essentially there are two ways to accommodate proposal information within your relationship management system:

1. *Multiple proposals:* If you anticipate a situation where your prospect may have multiple interests and may make multiple major gifts at or near the same time, you will need to have some of the rating information described earlier be associated with the proposal, not the prospect. For example, assigned solicitor, readiness, target ask, and target ask date would apply to the specific proposal, not the prospect.

2. *Singular proposals:* If your prospects will be making only one major gift at a time, or your shop is small, you do not run the risk of confusing the prospect with multiple proposals. In this case, you would only ever have one proposal open at a time, even if it represents a split gift. If your database does not have a separate proposal module or section, you might choose to record the proposal as an action.

Whichever situation applies to your organization, remember that having a target ask amount and target ask date recorded when the prospect is first assigned is an important way to keep your own internal sense of urgency pressuring you to stay on track to the gift.

Creating Reports to Track Progress

Reports from your relationship management system tell you if you are meeting your fundraising goals. Decide on the questions you want to have answered and then develop the reports to answer those questions.

There are three main areas of reporting you may wish to consider:

1. *Action reports:* Keep track of each individual in your prospect pool.

2. *Prospect review meetings:* Manage the fundraising team around prospects, provide a forum to brainstorm cultivation ideas and resolve assignment conflicts, and build internal skills.

3. *Executive review or reporting to goals:* Review overall progress toward fundraising goals.

By committing yourself to the discipline of regular reporting and review, you will be creating a culture of major-gift success in your organization. This prospect research function will contribute significantly toward your organization's ability to raise funds for its mission.

In his book *Fundraising Analytics: Using Data to Guide Strategy*, Joshua Birkholz calls upon his years and experience as a consultant to make the following statement:

> *The most successful fundraising institutions have solid prospect management programs. Organizations that seemingly out-raise their potential have dedicated systems focused on their constituents. The entire organization revolves around the prospect relationship.*

Relationship management is the one point of overlap between back-end support and frontline work that directly propels frontline fundraisers to ask for gifts. The discipline of relationship management combined with the skill of frontline fundraisers is the perfect recipe for receiving major gifts.

Action Reports   You will likely want to view your "to-do" list of actions on a regular basis. This is true whether you are a dedicated major-gift officer or an executive director in a grassroots organization. You may have actions to accomplish every day or only once a week. Either way, you need some way to remind yourself.

If your actions are recorded in the donor database, you may have the option to have actions that are not completed and due appear on your dashboard or home page. Usually this requires you to open the database software to view your actions. Some systems may also remind you via e-mail. You may decide to use this action listing every day, or you may want to print a report that lists your actions for the week. If there is a

Action Report for J. Jenkins

Due Date	Prospect Name	Type	Subject	Comments
2/15/2013	Sir James Chettam	Stewardship	Office vistit	He is going to give me a tour of his factory. Then lunch with the team that sponsored the project. Will present them with award.
3/12/2013	Humphrey Cadwallader	Cultivation	Lunch	Having lunch at his restaurant to discuss our food delivery program. We need news vans.
4/9/2013	Mary Garth	Solicitation	Home visit	She wants to sponsor a school program for a year. Taking board chair to review proposal with her.

FIGURE 4.3   **Action Report**

way to list your actions together with pertinent ratings such as capacity or readiness that will help keep you focused and motivated, this is even better! See Figure 4.3.

Hopefully all of your actions are recorded in the database. Even so, there are likely to be meetings and phone calls you will also need to have recorded in your calendar to be certain that you attend them.

Other Report Combinations   If you are not able to keep a relationship management system housed in your donor database, you may be keeping your top prospects listed in a spreadsheet or word processing document and your actions in your calendar. You will want to have the most current action date recorded with your prospect list as a way of ensuring that all of your prospects are being moved appropriately. Instead of printing a weekly report from your database, you may need to pick a day each week when you run down your list and update or review the action dates for each prospect.

Figure 4.4 is a sample of a prospect grid that includes planning and capturing actions, based on a template published online by the Public Broadcasting Major Giving Initiative.[2]

Prospect Review Meetings   It is a best practice to review your prospect list and update your ratings at regular intervals. You might schedule a weekly or monthly meeting among frontline fundraisers, prospect research staff and/or with your supervisor. Maybe it is a time you set aside on your own. There is not one best structure for prospect review meetings. The best practice is to conduct prospect review meetings that keep your major-gifts efforts moving forward. Almost by default, the discipline of regular prospect review meetings will encourage you to review and troubleshoot your strategies.

Even if you are a small or one-person shop and use a very simple relationship management system, regular, structured prospect review meetings can substitute for a more detailed relationship management system by keeping your prospects in front of you and your supervisor or board chair.

Setting the agenda requires a sharp focus on what needs to be accomplished in each meeting. You might concentrate on different tasks or on specific names as a way of limiting conversation to those prospects requiring strategy creation, troubleshooting, or assignment. For example, as you review the prospect pools, you might notice past due actions on highly rated prospects. Choosing those prospects for discussion forces evaluation and conversation before a major gift opportunity is lost.

Some common tasks accomplished during prospect review meetings include:

- Assignment of newly identified prospects.
- Outcomes of discovery/qualification visits.

---

[2]The Moves Management Prospect Grid was produced by The Public Broadcasting Major Giving Initiative (www.majorgivingnow.org) and was retrieved on June 8, 2012 from: www.majorgivingnow.org/downloads/xls/mm_grid.xls.

Prospect	Affinity	Prospect Stage	Capacity	Target Ask	Target Ask Date	Primary Volunteer	Interest	Next Action	Next Action
Sir James Chettam	Active	Stewardship	$50K–$100K	$10,000	8/15/12	Obama	Pie project	Tour and lunch	Stewardship report
Humphrey Cadwallader	Active	Cultivation	$100K–$500K	$150,000	6/30/13	Bush	Food vans	Lunch–get premission to ask	Ask b/f FY-end
Mary Garth	Insider	Solicitation	$500K–$1MM	$500,000	4/9/13	Clinton	School program	Review proposal-ask	CEO mtg for recognition

FIGURE 4.4   **Relationship Management in Excel**

- Creation of cultivation and solicitation strategies.
- Troubleshooting problems in identifying, qualifying, cultivating, and soliciting.

Prospect review meetings give you advantages such as:

- An atmosphere of teamwork that can foster creative brainstorming of strategies, sharing of insights, and skill-building.
- A chance to review the big picture of all major-gift prospects, deciding what is working and what is not.
- Discussion and assignment of new prospects and discussion about disqualifying prospects.
- The opportunity to address any specific issues relating to your major-gifts team, such as:
  - Are prospect pools getting too large to manage effectively?
  - Are the prospect pools not well distributed among staff?
  - Are other duties keeping frontline fundraisers from moving prospects forward?

If possible, prospect review meetings should be kept short. Many frontline fundraisers have horror stories about sitting through mind-numbing hours while everyone rambles on about their visits.

You may decide to meet weekly, monthly, or quarterly. Try out different intervals before settling on the meeting frequency that works. Choosing the same date and time each month helps everyone avoid scheduling conflicts and makes the expectation of attendance clear.

> To create momentum from your prospect review meetings, focus your agenda on making decisions that require actions. For example, if a new prospect is assigned, it should be clear that the prospect now needs information entered into the database, a discovery visit, and an action recorded. Time to get moving!

However you decide to run your prospect review meetings, you will need a report or list of your prospects with key information so that you can see and review the whole prospect pool. Ideally this will be a report created in the database that is easy to print so that you always have the most current information. See Figure 4.5.

If you were in a meeting reviewing the prospect review report in Figure 4.5, you might hear questions such as the following:

- Why hasn't Tertius Lydgate been assigned to a gift officer yet?
- Did Will Ladislaw respond to the tour? What is your next step?
- Are you having trouble getting a meeting with Edward Casaubon? It's been three months!
- Are you confident you will be asking by October?

Figure 4.6 illustrates a simple workflow for a prospect review meeting. You might have a standard agenda, or you might create a new agenda for each meeting. You might have specialized roles for relationship management, prospect research, and frontline fundraising, or you might have two people involved in the entire process. It all depends upon the number of staff you have, the size of your prospect pool, and your organization's needs.

Executive Review or Reporting to Goals Leadership responsible for setting fundraising and performance goals needs a method for periodically reviewing progress throughout the year. This usually takes on special importance when reporting to donors, the board of directors, and the public on campaign progress. Consider the following scenarios as examples of what strategic questions leadership may ask. Thinking ahead about what questions need to be answered leads you to record the right information in a way that can be easily reported.

If your goal is to raise a certain number of dollars from major gifts, and you have identified a pool of prospects, you might want to know:

- How many prospects are ready to give and what is the total amount we are likely to receive?
  - If you are tracking readiness and target ask, at any point in time, you can say what gifts you are likely to receive. Then you will know how close you are to reaching your goal.

Prospect Review Report

Prospect Name	Rating	Capacity Range	Prospect Stage	Ask Amt.	Ask Date	Last Action	Action Subject	Lead Staff
Tertius Lydgate	A	$10 million+	Identification			1/16/13	Researched	
Will Ladislaw	A	$1 million–$5 million	Cultivation	$500,000	1/31/14	3/22/13	Toured program	Bush
Rosamond Vincy	A	$500,000–$1 million	Qualification	$750,000	4/14/14	10/14/12	Schedule mtg	Clinton
Mary Garth	C	$500,000–$1 million	Solicitation	$350,000	4/25/12	4/5/13	Schedule mtg	Obama
Edward Casaubon	B	$100,000–$500,000	Cultivation	$150,000	10/31/13	1/4/13	Meet director	Bush

FIGURE 4.5 Prospect Review Report

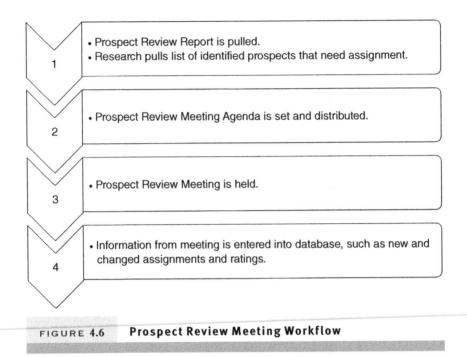

1
• Prospect Review Report is pulled.
• Research pulls list of identified prospects that need assignment.

2
• Prospect Review Meeting Agenda is set and distributed.

3
• Prospect Review Meeting is held.

4
• Information from meeting is entered into database, such as new and changed assignments and ratings.

FIGURE 4.6   **Prospect Review Meeting Workflow**

If your goal is to make six to eight substantial actions in one month, you want to know:

- Did a specific frontline fundraiser record actions on rated prospects in a calendar month?
  - If you are tracking solicitor assignments, actions, and some kind of prospect rating, you will know if the visits were made and what level of prospects were visited.

Figures 4.7 and 4.8 are examples of executive reports that might be used in a development shop with the director of development

Progress Toward Goals as of March 31, 2013
Fiscal Year-End 12/31/2013

	Planned Ask	Pending Asks	Accepted	Declined	Projected Total	2013 Goal	% of Goal Reached
Major Gifts Officer	$1,250,000	$125,000	$350,000	$30,000	$1,725,000	$1,000,000	48%
Development Director	$750,000	$10,000	$150,000	$0	$910,000	$600,000	27%
Totals	$2,000,000	$135,000	$500,000	$30,000	$2,635,000	$1,600,000	40%

(Note: % of Goal counts Pending and Accepted Asks)

FIGURE 4.7   **Progress Toward Goals**

and one gift officer tasked with major-gifts fundraising. The executive director and board members might take part in cultivating and soliciting prospects, but it is the director of development and her major gifts officer who are responsible for guiding the relationships and tracking progress. These reports are focused on whether they will be able to meet their dollar goals and whether they are actively cultivating prospects with the highest capacity.

The "Progress Toward Goals" report in Figure 4.7 gives leadership a snapshot view of how close the organization is to its fundraising goal at the end of the first quarter. Did you notice how the total ask amount planned is greater than the goal? Not every prospect will give and not every prospect will give at the level asked. By aiming higher, this organization expects to reach or exceed its goals.

The "Solicitor Review" report in Figure 4.8 shows how long prospects have been sitting in the prospect pool. This kind of report will highlight when a prospect is not moving as expected through the gift cycle. Did you notice that Dorothea Brooke is still in the qualification stage after six months? Given her rating, "B" for high affinity/low capacity, we might wonder why she hasn't moved into the cultivation stage.

Solicitor Review: B.Obama
As of 3/31/13

Assigned 1 to 6 months: Identification and Qualification

Prospect Name	Rating	Capacity Range	Prospect Stage	Ask Amt	Ask Date	Last Action	Action Subject
Tertius Lydgate	A	$10 million+	Identification			1/6/13	Researched
Rosamond Vincy	A	$500,000–$1 million	Qualification	$750,000	4/14/14	10/14/12	Schedule mtg

Assigned 6 to 12 months: Cultivation

Prospect Name	Rating	Capacity Range	Prospect Stage	Ask Amt	Ask Date	Last Action	Action Subject
Dorothea Brooke	B	$10,000–$50,000	Qualification	$5,000	11/10/13	8/25/12	Discovery call
Will Ladislaw	A	$1million–$5 million	Cultivation	$500,000	1/31/14	3/22/13	Toured program

Assigned 12 to 18 months: Cultivation and Solicitation

Prospect Name	Rating	Capacity Range	Prospect Stage	Ask Amt	Ask Date	Last Action	Action Subject
Edward Casaubon	B	$100,000–$500,000	Cultivation	$150,000	10/31/13	1/4/13	Meet director

Assigned 18+ months

Prospect Name	Rating	Capacity Range	Prospect Stage	Ask Amt	Ask Date	Last Action	Action Subject
Mary Garth	C	$500,000–$1 million	Solicitation	$350,000	4/25/12	4/5/13	Schedule ask mtg

FIGURE 4.8   **Solicitor Review**

Creating and maintaining a relationship management system requires an attention to detail and discipline that can be burdensome to an overwhelmed fundraiser, but it's critical to your success.

Following are real-life examples of relationship management systems being used in organizations of different sizes and with different needs to give you inspiration. Remember, the goal of a relationship management system is to help you achieve a higher level of fundraising success. If it does not do that, then it is time to make changes. Creating a system that works for you takes time and effort, but it's worth it.

BRILLIANTLY SIMPLE SOLUTION BY INGRID ZEPP, DIRECTOR, ADVANCEMENT OPERATIONS AT URSINUS COLLEGE

When I was National Director, Database Management & Research at the Devereux Foundation, I had the challenge of devising a prospect management system that could be used by all of its facilities around the country. Because each facility had different needs and abilities, I needed to keep the system simple, but still keep our major gift efforts moving forward.

Although the Raiser's Edge database in use by Devereux had the prospect module, I decided to keep three key items in attributes. Keeping everything in one place made it especially easy for people to enter the information. We tracked capacity rating, target gift amount, and solicitation phase. If a capacity rating was entered by the fundraiser, the prospect's record would pull in a customized report. (Other ratings from vendors were stored in the prospect module and did not require any user action.)

We continued to use the usual entry in Raiser's Edge for actions, assigned solicitors, and proposals. Creating a solicitation strategy and recording it in a constituent note on the record was encouraged, but not required.

With this combination of tracking, it was easy to train all of the development staff and the national office was able to keep track of the major gift efforts nationwide.

(Continued)

A Work in Progress by Debbie Sokolov, Director of Development, St. Petersburg Free Clinic

Soon after I started at the St. Petersburg Free Clinic we hired a prospect research consultant to come in and help us with our major gifts initiative. As I was putting together the fundraising plan and attempting to familiarize myself with the 16,000 donors in our system, the consultant was busy looking inside our database and segmenting our donors. It really gave us a jump-start on identifying our best major-gift prospects.

Once we reviewed the list, adding and subtracting names, we created a plan for each of our top prospects and a system for tracking the information. Doing this made us more mindful and responsible for major gifts. Now we can focus on our best prospects and stay on task with each individual we have identified. Even though there are just two of us, the executive director and me, we have begun meeting each month to review our prospects and will be creating some additional reports to make sure we are progressing on time to our goal.

It felt like a lot of additional work at first, but it actually has saved me time. Now my prospect pool is defined and manageable. I can keep a concentrated focus on moving prospects to a gift. I don't have to keep spinning my wheels with prospects who are not able to give at the level we need. We are still a work in progress, but we are definitely making progress with major gifts. It has been worth the effort and the proof is in the numbers.

Communication is Key by Mary Jamieson Dee, Director, Prospect Research at the University of North Florida

The research team at the University of North Florida works closely with approximately 15 fundraisers, including members of central staff, to ensure that prospects move effectively through the pipeline. The Institutional Advancement development staff meets biweekly to discuss recent gifts and proposals, and research meets quarterly with gift officers to review prospects who haven't been contacted in 12 months. During these meetings, we work together to determine whether more research is needed on these prospects, whether fundraisers need an additional six months to meet with prospects, whether the prospect might be a better fit for another unit of the University, or whether the prospect should be placed back into the pool. Research also highlights those prospects assigned for discovery and the reason for the assignment. These processes help fundraisers work with a manageable number of prospects.

Development officers also enter proposals on the prospect tab in Raiser's Edge. A prospect can have multiple proposals, so we track the status, ask amount, target ask date, and other items on each proposal. We also review active proposals to ascertain if proposal statuses need updating, and in many cases, as those statuses change, we update the prospect status accordingly. In addition, Research reviews contact reports on a regular basis and updates prospect statuses accordingly. For example, if it is clear that a prospect has moved from discovery to cultivation, we will make that change. In the cases where it is less clear, we contact the gift officer.

Our system works well and we are winding up a successful campaign, but I always have ideas for improvement. For example, I plan to develop a stage-aging report that could show how long prospects are in each stage.

Summary

The purpose of a relationship management system is to solicit and close on more and larger gifts. A system facilitates this through the intertwined movement of three major groups of tasks:

1. Ratings to stay focused on the best prospects.
2. A record of the actual moves made with prospects.
3. Reports to stay on task and allow for strategic review and decision making.

Implementing and maintaining a strong relationship management system requires additional work for the fundraising team, but the reward is higher giving.

There are as many different ways to manage prospects as there are nonprofit organizations. Whether you are starting from scratch or reviewing your current system, understanding what you want to know will direct you to what you should record. For example, if you want to answer how many prospects are ready to make a gift of $500,000 or more before the fiscal year end, then you need to be sure you are tracking target gift amount, target gift date, and gift readiness.

Identifying your prospects and managing them with a system will bring you a long way towards major gift success, but there is still one more aspect of prospect research you need to help you close on significant gifts. Doing individual research on your prospects will give you a distinct edge in maximizing your actual gift size.

In the next chapter we describe the different levels of research you might consider, what is included in a typical donor prospect profile, and the resources you might want to purchase. We will also equip you with some basic search techniques every fundraiser should know.

FOR FURTHER READING

Burnett, Ken. *Relationship Fundraising: A Donor-Based Approach to the Business of Raising Money.* San Francisco, CA: Jossey-Bass, 2002.

Hedrick, Janet. *Effective Donor Relations.* Hoboken, NJ: John Wiley & Sons, 2008.

Strand, Bobbie. *A Kaleidoscope of Prospect Development: The Shapes and Shades of Major Donor Prospecting.* Washington, DC: Council for Advancement and Support of Education (CASE), 2008.

Sturtevant, William T. *The Artful Journey: Cultivating and Soliciting the Major Gift.* Chicago: Bonus, 1997.

CHAPTER 5

Managing Prospect Research

The most important thing to me is that fundraisers should ask for and expect strategic information, as opposed to comprehensive information, and that in order to provide strategic info, researchers need feedback and should not be expected to work in a vacuum.

—ANDREA BALZANO, Prospect Researcher, Resource
Development Group, Enterprise Community Partners

It is not uncommon for a front-line fundraiser to be charged with managing a prospect research employee or department. For many who have not been prospect researchers themselves, how research is done can be a mystery. You may not be aware of what prospect researchers can find, or the breadth or limitations of resources available. You may have the luxury of working with a team of experienced researchers who understand fundraising strategy, or have just hired someone who has never done research before.

The challenge for you, the supervisor, is to communicate the organization's fundraising goals, take the time to talk with your researcher to decide what research strategies will meet those goals, and provide adequate training opportunities and resources so that they can do the best job possible. Your researcher or research team will need to learn new techniques, benchmark with other organizations about best practices, and bring the information back to you so that you can decide whether you should make changes or try something new.

This chapter talks about hiring staff and what skills to look for, as well as where a prospect researcher might report on an organization chart. We also discuss training needs and talk about purchasing resources. And because so many organizations are not ready for full-time research staff, we have collected case studies on how prospect research can be outsourced and used effectively in the small office.

MANAGING TO YOUR FUNDRAISING GOALS

If you are in charge of managing prospect research in your organization, it is up to you to match your fundraising priorities with research. What does that mean? It means that you must find the appropriate tool or method at a price you can afford, that will lead you to the fundraising results you need. Let's walk through two examples of the same goal, but in very different organizations.

CASE STUDY

IMPROVING MAJOR-GIFTS INITIATIVES USING PROSPECT RESEARCH

This text will be removed during the revision of proofs, but I wanted to include something so that if a sentence or short paragraph is inserted it does not require reflow of the text.

HUMAN SERVICES GROUP

Human Services Group has been successfully attracting annual gifts from donors in the amount of $10,000 or more without any dedicated effort for major gifts. HSG's leadership has decided it is time to expand some of the organization's programs and renovate some of the buildings. To do this, you, as Director of Development, have been charged with pursuing more major gifts, including planned gifts and pledges.

You receive authorization and hire a full-time gift officer who previously worked as a gift officer at a large university.

She needs more prospects than are currently identified, so you purchase a wealth screening. Your database manager is very skilled, and he works closely with the vendor. As soon as the screening results are in the database, you and your team begin reviewing reports and assigning prospects. The gift officer begins calling prospects. Once she confirms a prospect's interest and is moving toward a solicitation, she orders a prospect profile from a consultant. Because of the new focus on the most capable and interested donors, timely research, and a professional approach, the gift officer exceeds her goal in the first year.

GENERAL HOSPITAL FOUNDATION

General Hospital Foundation employs three major gift officers who have become concerned about the size and quality of their prospect pools. It has been three years since the last electronic wealth screening, and the system for screening patients has not been producing the leads expected. The president has been hinting that there might be a new campaign in a couple of years.

As Vice President of Development, you decide to hire a prospect research consultant to audit current efforts and make recommendations. She recommends (a) a wealth screening on a subset of records, (b) creating a standard procedure for the review of new prospects, (c) assigning the daily patient screening results to the prospect researcher to review, and (c) creating relationship management policies that address how a new prospect is assigned and managed. It takes a year and a half, but by the time the campaign plans are finalized, the fundraising effort is running much more smoothly and efficiently.

As you can see from these examples, even the same tools can be used differently to meet different needs. The human services group had a comparatively small set of donors and screened all of them. The hospital targeted a subset of records to immediately address gift officer needs, but also anticipated new prospects from patient screenings. Also, notice how the hospital used a prospect research consultant for direction even though it had a prospect researcher on staff. With the pressure of a pending campaign, the hospital needed to become

(Continued)

more effective sooner rather than later, and the fundraising manager knew changes take time to implement. You can use prospect research tools like electronic screenings to have work performed for you, such as prioritizing your prospect pool, and you can use a prospect research consultant to boost your organization's internal capacity to perform its own research tasks through consulting or by providing another skilled pair of hands when needed.

When planning for a campaign, leadership should consider that it is not uncommon to see a shift in research priorities during the life of a campaign. Emphasis on prospect identification and qualification is heavy during the planning phases to create a population of strong candidates to support major gift activity.

A solid relationship management system coupled with strong analytical and data interpretation components help to sustain this base. Shifting gears to strategic thinking and applying in-depth researching methods at the right time is crucial through the close of a campaign. These components cry for different resources at different times.

Maintain a flexible budget and maximize on the skillset of a seasoned staff to adapt seamlessly to the evolving needs of a fundraising campaign environment.

—NANCY M. LEE, Prospect Research Consultant and Director
for Donor Services, Jefferson Foundation,
Thomas Jefferson University and Hospitals

As Part of Everyone's Job

In a very small fundraising department, prospect research becomes a part of everyone's job, with direction coming from the lead fundraiser. Figure 5.1 shows the Director of Development in the center driving common prospect research tasks. In this scenario, it is important to assign tasks based on each employee or volunteer's interests and skill set. For example:

- If a staff member is excited to discover prospect information and has developed some skill at it, why not encourage her and ensure the information is recorded so it can be retrieved?

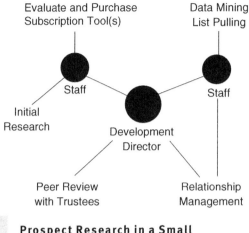

FIGURE 5.1   **Prospect Research in a Small Development Office**

- If your gift entry staff member is always making subtle connections between gifts and donors, such as noticing when a business gift should be connected to the business owner who is also a donor or prospect, why not see if he would be interested in running some reports to answer strategic questions?

In a small office, it is up to the Director of Development to understand which questions and answers will move the entire fundraising effort forward. Decide on the benchmarks you want to track and assign prospect research tasks that achieve those benchmarks. For example, you might come up with a core set of questions along the lines of the following:

- *Events:* How many major-gift prospects were identified at our fundraising events and are now being cultivated?
  - If you are running special events of any kind, consider adding prospect identification of businesses and individuals to the evaluation. Special events already require a highly organized individual. Your staff member might have great ideas about this!

- *Annual fund:* Did we evaluate and act upon annual fund donors for higher gift amounts and planned gifts?
  - So often we focus on the total dollar amount. If you are already pulling reports to determine the success of your annual appeals, why not add some reports that look at individuals who increased their giving, or now have consecutive giving for a certain number of years?
- *Board development:* How many prospect visits did our board members initiate and/or attend?
  - It can take a lot of effort to begin involving board members, but the rewards are well documented. Your Executive Director/CEO is usually the best placed staff member to manage and encourage board member participation.
- *Major gifts:* What is a major gift for our organization? And how many prospects were asked for a major gift?
  - Even if your major gift is still an unrestricted annual gift at a certain amount or above, you need a way to track success with your largest donors. Can you create a development committee on the board charged with reviewing the major donor list periodically?
- *Stewardship:* Which stewardship efforts resulted in the most donor activity or response?
  - Strong stewardship is like electricity. We don't notice it until it stops working. Who likes tinkering in your database? That person will find an easy way to attach each individual record with all mailings sent, events attended, and other information. Now you can begin to look at correlations between your stewardship activities, communication efforts and giving.

In a smaller shop, you expect your development efforts to be rewarded with consistent growth. As your organization begins raising more money and growing its programs, it will also begin investing in more fundraising staff to accommodate this growth. Every organization has different needs, but hiring a dedicated prospect researcher does not usually happen until there is significant potential for major gifts, including a full-time gift officer.

Major gifts offer the highest return on investment for the cost of a prospect research staff member. Organizations receiving $2 million to as high as $10 million in gifts annually might outsource some or all of their prospect research needs. Consultants and vendors can assist with specific projects, such as the following:

- Improving fundraising performance through donor segmentation, analysis, and testing.
- Identifying major-gift prospects.
- Implementing a donor relationship management system.
- Donor profiling.

As your organization moves beyond large annual gifts into major and planned gifts and demand for prospect research swells, it is important to keep a close watch on the cost-effectiveness of contracted services. For example, if the cost of your purchase or contract exceeds the amount of money you anticipate raising through gifts, you might be buying a solution that is too big for your current needs. Alternatively, you may want to make a larger initial investment to begin building internal capacity.

CASE STUDY

Chosen Charity's fundraising efforts were successful and growing fast. The executive director had just signed a contract to bring a consultant in to implement a new donor acquisition strategy. As part of the contract, the database manager would be trained on how to analyze the acquisition/direct-appeal performance and would assume this responsibility in the second year.

The database manager was finding it difficult to manage the gift entry and acknowledgments and keep up with the current demands for evaluating direct appeals and other reporting. Chosen Charity decided to hire a gift entry clerk to perform some of the tasks.

As a result of its investment in both a consultant and additional staff, Chosen Charity grew its internal capacity and made efficient use of consulting services.

Once you are receiving $5 million to $10 million or more in annual, individual gifts, you are likely to have a specialized database manager and one or more frontline fundraisers dedicated to major and planned gifts. At this point, the need for prospect research tasks likely increases to the point where having a well-trained prospect researcher on staff is necessary.

As a Standalone Department or Staff Member

An organization in which prospect research is beginning to evolve into a separate function or even its own department altogether will have to answer the question, "Who should the prospect research team report to?" The usual choices are the head of development or the head of operations. The best choice might be either!

In the past, prospect research was known almost exclusively for simply gathering data. This was in the form of printing reports from the database or compiling information on prospects. Prospect research pushed information out into the development arena. Like gift entry and other advancement services, a prospect researcher would not always have had regular interaction with the frontline fundraising staff. The information was often collected in the same way: without too much consideration for changing needs.

Today, the prospect researcher has evolved into the position of development partner. Inundated with information, the development department relies upon prospect research to provide strategic information and work in partnership with frontline fundraisers to provide real-time data. More than in the past, prospect researchers are recognized as fundraisers too, understanding development principles and directing front-line staff to exactly the information they need. Prospect research also creates and maintains donor relationship management systems and introduces and assimilates new technologies to provide an organization with competitive advantages.

As Mark Knoll, Associate Vice President of Advancement Services at Kansas State University Foundation, says, prospect research really sits on the fence between operations and development. As head of the prospect research department, he reports to the Senior Vice President of Development, but he has a dotted line to the Executive Director. This gives him the benefit of reporting to someone who is deeply entrenched in fundraising, but the opportunity to appeal to the operations team when there is a conflict or he needs support dealing with an area like information technology. No matter where a prospect research team reports, researchers need to interact very closely with their development colleagues on the front line as well as the IT team or database manager.

HIRING EMPLOYEES AND VOLUNTEERS

Employees

As mentioned, management frequently begins to consider hiring a prospect researcher on staff when there are dedicated gift officers eager for more prospects in their portfolios and more information about those potential donors. This is often when individual giving is $5 million or higher, but varies greatly among organizations.

You might find yourself exploring whether you want to add additional duties to an existing employee—maybe someone involved in the maintenance of your donor data—or create an entirely new position. Of course, these decisions are unique to the goals of your organization and fundraising department, but there are some general ways in which you might assess the value a prospect researcher could bring to your fundraising efforts.

We know that prospect research answers questions of importance to fundraising in three major areas:

1. Finding new prospects.
2. Qualifying existing prospects.
3. Donor relationship management.

Underlying these areas is the need for the prospect research person or team to lead the department in overall data management. Whether you have or create multiple positions under prospect research or add duties to another position, following are some performance benchmarks you might consider:

- Number of new prospects over a period of time that you need to have identified, qualified, and assigned to a gift officer for cultivation.
- Number of donor prospects profiled over a period of time.
- Dollars given by profiled prospects over a period of time.
- Ability to provide reporting from the donor database to inform strategy.

As you can see in Table 5.1, before you hire, you might consider whether you can create some internal capacity by assigning some tasks to existing employees and outsourcing other tasks. Outsourcing data analysis or profiling can be cost-effective in the right situations, particularly for special needs like event briefings or other short-term/quick turnaround needs. You will get expert services as needed, without employee, software subscription, and training costs.

TABLE 5.1	Employee Needs Analysis
Time Required	**Hours/Cost**
Major gift prospect pool: 75	
Expected solicitations in a year: 10	
Estimated deep research profiles: 10 prospect profiles × 8 hours	80 hours
Estimated capacity qualification profiles: 20 prospect profiles × 2 hours	40 hours
Data mining to identify new prospects	10 hours
Data-based evaluation of direct appeal efforts	32 hours
Administrative time (meetings, e-mail, timesheet)	20 hours
Total likely prospect research employee hours, assuming 35 hours/week	182 hours or 5.2 weeks
Average prospect research salary (APRA, 2012) (This does not include benefits, taxes, training or any other employee costs.)	$56,000/year or $31/hour
Overhead costs 30 to 40 percent	$16,800–$22,400
Estimate of basic prospect research subscription costs (per researcher)	$5,000–$10,000+/year

If you have a more mature prospect research department, hiring new employees with specific expertise—such as data analysis, a business research background, or proficiency in the language of your largest international population—could give you power to boost your philanthropic dollars significantly.

The challenge is to balance an organization's budgetary need for people to ask for major gifts with the capacity of a prospect research team to support them. The ratio of gift officers to prospect researchers varies greatly among organizations. You might expect one prospect researcher to support anywhere from three to eight major gift officers. The wide range reflects differences in organization size and demand for research. According to the 2012 APRA Salary Survey, the average ratio of researchers to front-line fundraisers is 1:6.

As we will discuss in more detail under the upcoming heading "Skill Sets for Hiring," achieving competency in the various tasks under the prospect research umbrella takes time and training. If you begin assigning prospect research duties to existing staff or hire a dedicated prospect researcher, you will need to be committed to providing them with initial and ongoing training. You probably would not feel safe in a house built by an untrained carpenter. Likewise, a prospect researcher with little or no training will not deliver consistently meaningful information, the kind needed to properly evaluate and help make decisions about your fundraising strategies.

If you are looking to create more structure around prospect research tasks and techniques, consider hiring someone who has worked in a more complex prospect research department, such as higher education. You will pay a higher salary, but the researcher's prior experience will add benefit to your major-gifts program quickly.

If you are just beginning to need prospect research, consider adding prospect research to a staff member responsible for the database or annual fund, or hiring someone to add value to those areas as well as doing prospect research. You will pay a lower salary for little or no experience, but you will need to spend money on training.

Volunteers

Inviting volunteers to participate in prospect research tasks can be very rewarding for the volunteers and for you. Whether you create an intern position for students (paid or unpaid), find someone who wants to gain new workplace skills, or engage any other kind of volunteer, there are a number of tasks well-suited to volunteers.

Before we discuss specific tasks, how you train your volunteers is an important consideration. In Chapter 6 we will discuss ethics and legal risks in prospect research. Treating volunteers as employees, albeit unpaid, creates the atmosphere of respect for your donors and your donors' data. Providing volunteers with an introduction to fundraising, an understanding of where prospect research fits into the picture, and training in how to perform their tasks legally and ethically, as well as having them sign a confidentiality agreement, lays the proper groundwork for a successful volunteer relationship and reduces risk for your organization.

Depending upon the size and scope of your fundraising efforts, you might have a volunteer:

- *Create and scan news alerts and local periodicals for prospects.* You might be looking for alumni or you might be looking for keywords related to your mission.
- *Perform initial qualification research.* You might develop a checklist for a large or small prospect identification project, such as having the volunteer qualify names by home market value and past gifts to you or other organizations at or above certain values.
- *Do routine address and phone look-up.* When envelopes are returned as undeliverable or when you are trying to flesh out mailing addresses, phone numbers, and e-mail addresses, you might consider having a volunteer look up the information online for you.

We know that most high schools in our area require students to complete community service hours, so we recruit these computer-savvy students to do address look-ups for us. If mail is returned or we otherwise need contact information, they search out the most current information and check to make sure the person is not deceased.

—LAURA BREEZE, CFRE, Advancement Director at the Education Foundation of Sarasota County

SKILL SETS FOR HIRING

The Association of Professional Researchers for Advancement (APRA) (www.aprahome.org) has put together skill sets for different levels of prospect researchers and different positions within the field. Whether you are hiring for a position within an existing prospect research department or starting one from scratch, these are a valuable aid in your hiring. In them you will find detail on the types of tasks and skills required at each level. Because the field of prospect research and the technologies available for data creation and management have been changing rapidly, this book will focus on the underlying characteristics that are common in great researchers.

It was not so many years ago that a college degree in nonprofit management or fundraising did not exist.[1] People often "fell into" fundraising from different areas of an organization or the for-profit sector. The same holds true for prospect researchers. As of this writing, there is no higher education major or minor dedicated to training prospect researchers.

As you think about the information needs for your organization, we encourage you to be creative and get the best—not just the most—from your investment of time and money in prospect research.

---

[1]Some universities offer a track in nonprofit management as part of their existing graduate programs, but in June of 2012, The Indiana University Board of Trustees approved the formation of a School of Philanthropy to be located on the Indiana University-Purdue University Indianapolis campus. (Reported on 7/12/2012 from: www.philanthropy.iupui.edu/news/2012/06/pr-IUTrusteesApproveSchool ofPhilanthropyPlan.aspx.)

Following are some characteristics to look for in a future prospect research employee and possible interview questions:

- *Analytical:* Someone who is curious how past information could be used to make decisions in the future, who searches for patterns in what otherwise seems a jumble, and who is able to put information in an order that is usable.
  - *Sample interview question:* Have you ever made suggestions for changing a process or system that resulted in an improvement?
- *Able to scan for relevant information:* Someone who knows the fundraising fundamentals and can provide more and better information without spending too much time on information that will not lead toward a gift.
  - *Sample interview question:* Provide two news articles that contain biographical, wealth, and philanthropic giving information about a prominent individual. Ask the interviewee to synthesize the information in a brief memorandum.
- *Able to write and summarize well:* Summarizing reams of information on a high-profile philanthropist is no easy task, but relaying it in an easy-to-read format is just as important. A skilled researcher cuts to the quick and clearly outlines what is important to know.
  - *Sample interview question:* Ask the interviewee to summarize an article on a high-profile philanthropist in a limited number of sentences.
- *Discerning:* Online information sources often appear authoritative, but are not; news articles and social media are full of opinions, not facts; and even court documents can include family feud gossip. A good researcher can tell the difference and include what is appropriate.
  - *Sample interview question:* You just read in a blog that a prospect you are researching has conspired with politicians to gain business fraudulently. What do you do next?
- *Creative:* Research is not linear. If someone must complete #1 and #2 before completing #3, they probably won't be a good fit.

Many times the ability to leap from #1 to #5 and back to #2 is the only way to gather critical information.

- *Sample interview question:* In a list of real-estate records, your prospect's address is used by an owner with a different name. What do you do?
- *Independent:* Prospect research requires a lot of time in front of a computer screen making multiple decisions every minute. You want someone who knows when to make decisions on her own and when to ask for help.
  - *Sample interview question:* Tell me about a project that you initiated on your own without anyone telling you what to do.
- *Donor-centric:* A good prospect researcher is also a fundraiser and answers her own internal questions when researching, such as: Why did the prospect make that gift to XYZ Charity?
  - *Sample interview question:* Can you give an example of a time when you provided a key piece of information that helped a frontline fundraiser connect with a prospect?
- *Able to collaborate and communicate:* Having an employee that can collaborate on projects and communicate clearly with others is important no matter what the position.
  - *Sample interview question:* Describe a work-related incident that was stressful for you and how you handled it.

If you find that your current research staff lack some of these characteristics or have some gaps in their knowledge, training can be very helpful. However, you may find that some people are simply not comfortable operating in a more strategic setting and training might not be able to overcome this reluctance.

As you are looking over resumes, you might consider that according to the APRA 2012 Salary Survey Report:

- Forty-nine percent of members held a bachelor's degree and 37 percent held a master's degree.
- Average salaries vary across the United States, with the highest median salaries paid in the Northeast ($61,000) and the lowest

in the Midwest ($51,000). The median salary for a prospect researcher in Canada was reported to be $50,000.

Work experience that translates well to prospect research includes the following:

- Library sciences.
- Law, such as legal secretary and paralegal.
- Marketing, especially market research.
- Writing and technical positions.
- Positions involving data technology and process.

MANAGING EXPECTATIONS

Ever since Google made search engines indispensable, our perception of research has changed. Suddenly the answer to any question seems within easy clicking—just Google it! However, with the floodgates to information wide open, skilled researchers have become even more valuable. As a frontline fundraiser, do you really have time to get lost in a search engine for hours trying to find information about your prospect because you didn't know which specific website to visit? Did you know that approximately 90 percent of what is on the Internet cannot be found in search engines?

A skilled researcher finds information quickly because she knows the following:

- How to use a search engine effectively.
- Which resources must be accessed directly or with a password.
- Whether the information she wants to find is likely to be found online, offline, or not at all.

When you hire a prospect researcher without previous direct experience, it is important to provide training on the art and science of fundraising as well as how to find the information being sought. When you hire an experienced prospect researcher, you may find that someone expert in donor profiling may have no understanding of data analytics and vice versa.

Research finds answers to questions and informs strategy; it is a nonlinear skill. Instead of traveling in a straight line, a prospect researcher might search in many directions at any one time. That means that even if you started with a standard list of sources to be checked, it will change for each question to be answered. For example, I may begin each prospect profile with a name and home address and my favorite deep web information subscription, but I may need to jump to a different website to check a fact or confirm a current status before returning to the subscription information and continuing down my list of resources.

Because of this "jumping around," becoming an expert at prospect research takes time and practice to learn when, what, where, and how to find information that will lead to increased giving. Add to this environment the constantly and quickly changing technologies and you come to understand why someone without training and/or who is expected to turn around research in a very short period of time might deliver disappointing results.

CASE STUDY

Julie has worked for a school of public health as a frontline fundraiser for many years. She was recently charged with creating a new advisory board for the school's department of health policy and management. Members of this board would be drawn from a specific industry, and a major-gift donation would be an expectation of board membership.

"I met with our researcher John and told him I needed a new group of names for this board, and he came back with a list of alumni from that department! They don't have major-gift capacity and it was just a useless list. I thought he'd know what I needed but I was really disappointed and frustrated.

"Fortunately, we have a pretty good relationship, so I asked him to try again. This time we sat down and went over the whole

(Continued)

project end to end. I realized that, although I meet with these industry leaders every day, John had no clue how they live, how they're really compensated, and how they're connected.

"Once I gave him the road map, the list got much better. We continue to refine it, and now I have the beginning of a strong advisory group. John's done a lot of research on that industry group now and proactively sends me names when he finds them."

DEFINING COMMON TERMS AND USING FORMS

Even if you have a skilled prospect researcher, you might get disappointing results if the researcher does not fully understand the request or if she has a different definition for common terms like "major gift."

Consider these requests a prospect researcher might receive and consider the questions that follow each:

- Please generate a list of major-gift prospects not already assigned to a frontline fundraiser.
  - What is a major gift? Five thousand dollars or $5 million?
- Please prepare a donor profile on this person.
  - What should go in a donor profile? Should I spend 1 hour or 10 hours on this request?
- Can you get me a list of the top companies in our city?
  - What is the purpose? What is a top company for our organization?

Whether you are just adding prospect research to your fundraising shop or already have dedicated staff, defining common terms is important.

As you learn more about specific tasks that fall under the big umbrella of prospect research, it will help you define things for your organization. In addition to defining common terms, you might consider creating some or all of the following forms:

- *Research request form:* Some research shops swear by their form; others have abolished forms to encourage researchers and frontline fundraisers to talk to each other. A research request form can also help the researcher ask the right questions to perform her job, and can help remind the frontline fundraiser to tie the level of her request to the prospect's stage in the gift cycle.
- *Donor profile templates:* Having a template ensures that the researcher knows what to include and the frontline fundraiser knows where to look. Here are some examples of common profile needs:
  - *Event briefs:* The short paragraph or bullet points to give to your president, board members, or others as conversation starters with donor prospects at an event.
  - *Identification, qualification, or snapshot profiles:* These are short profiles requested early in the cultivation process to be sure there is an inclination to give and enough wealth to give to warrant further resources.
  - *Cultivation profiles:* Once a prospect is qualified for wealth and interest, a cultivation profile can provide the details to pull the prospect closer to the organization.
  - *Solicitation or comprehensive profiles:* Usually requested to help prepare for a major gift proposal.
- *Checklists:* Common checklists used in prospect research are:
  - Checklists of sources that should be searched for nearly every prospect, especially including paid subscriptions.
  - Checklists of what and where information should be entered in the database.

Defining common terms and having some forms and checklists in place can keep operations running smoothly, but keep in mind that you need to remain flexible to meet the needs of your leadership and your organization overall. At least once in your career, you will receive a request for information from leadership that goes against established procedures. The president might demand a full and comprehensive profile every time he goes on a prospect visit or a board chair might wish to have a profile to review prior to visits. Following are some things you might consider as you respond to leadership:

- *If possible, ask sensitive questions about how the information will help the person requesting it.* It may be that your leadership is uncomfortable with visiting donors and having information gives her more confidence. You can craft a profile template that gives her confidence and makes best use of your staff's time. Uncovering the need behind the request can solve what appears at first to be a problem.

- *When board members are actively participating in donor cultivation and solicitation, they have a need for information.* Creating a format that informs them while still respecting the privacy of your prospect meets the needs of all parties.

- *Start with a "Yes!" when responding to leadership, but clarify the need.* For example, "Yes, we will definitely provide you with in-depth information prior to your meetings, but I'd like to be sure we give you the information you are expecting. Could we talk about what information you want in the profile?"

- *Do your best to understand the need behind what might appear to be an unreasonable request and do a good job of explaining the cost of the resources.* As you respond to inquiries, include descriptive information such as how long a profile takes to accomplish. For example, you might say the following: "Thank you for your request for a comprehensive profile. Would you please let me know the date of your visit? It takes anywhere from 6 to 12 hours to accomplish a comprehensive profile and I want to be sure we get it to you on time."

Supporting your researcher or research team by pre-empting unnecessary research requests from leadership will help you retain research staff and keep their time available for important requests.

PURCHASING RESOURCES

There are three overlapping categories of prospect research resources—search tools, analytics tools, and summary look-up tools—and there are

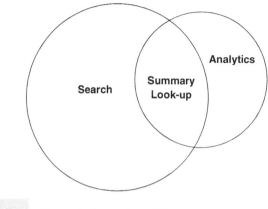

FIGURE 5.2   **Three Categories of Resources**

free and fee vendors in all categories. See Figure 5.2. You will find updated link lists and other resources at the online complement to this book at www.Research4Fundraisers.com.

Search Tools

Search tools help find deep information about individuals, companies, and foundations. The search tools you choose will depend upon the depth of research you intend to accomplish internally and the size of your organization's budget. With the exception of real estate, a rule of thumb is that a lot of information can be found through free sources, but a paid subscription will save you a lot of time. (There is no free source that allows you to search for real-estate ownership across multiple states, but many individual counties in many states let you search for free.)

There are hundreds of great subscription services and websites that can assist you in research. Because there are so many online sources for research and because they change so frequently, we encourage you to visit the companion website to this book, www.Research4 Fundraisers.com, for current lists of links and other resources. Although we have resources online for you, we couldn't resist including just a few of our favorite websites here.

As you discover your favorite websites, the ones you use the most often, you will probably want to bookmark them. Most people start out doing this on their Internet browser. If you find you are collecting a lot of bookmarks and it is getting unwieldy, consider trying an online bookmarking application like Delicious.com or Digg.com. Besides being able to organize your favorite websites more easily, these applications go wherever you go and allow you to share your favorites with others.

Our favorite paid subscriptions include the following:

- Foundation Center (www.foundationcenter.org), Foundation-Search America (www.foundationsearch.com), and Guidestar (www.guidestar.org)

    If you are searching for grant funding, you will want a subscription, although Foundation Center does offer its premium product free in select libraries. Paid subscriptions also allow you to search by name for directors and officers of foundations.
- Hoovers (www.hoovers.com) and Dun & Bradstreet (www.dnb.com)

    Both Hoovers and Dun & Bradstreet offer extensive information on private companies for a fee, but don't overlook the many private company and business subscriptions your local library may have.
- Highbeam Research (www.highbeam.com) and Factiva (www.dowjones.com/factiva/)

    These two resources, along with Lexis Nexis for Development Professionals, are the top three go-to resources for business and general news sources, from newspapers and magazines to white papers and press releases.
- iWave PRO (www.iwave.com) and LexisNexis for Development Professionals (LNDP; www.lexisnexis.com)

    These subscriptions allow you to search in different ways across multiple sources of public information, including company, and foundation information, philanthropic giving, news and more. LNDP and iWave, like Highbeam and Factiva are aggregators which allow you speed, flexibility and access to deeper resources.

- Knowx (www.knowx.com)

    Knowx was purchased by LexisNexis, but has been maintained as a separate subscription. It is not as powerful as LexisNexis, but it is easier to use, is less expensive, and has very flexible subscription options. Knowx provides access to information such as business/company information and public records.

- Morningstar (www.morningstar.com)

    Formerly known as 10K Wizard, Morningstar provides access to information (such as salary and holdings) about publicly-held companies and corporate insiders. The service allows you to create alerts for company events such as a sale or other big news.

- NOZA (www.nozasearch.com)

    NOZA allows you to search by a prospect's name for gifts made to charitable organizations. It also has some flexible subscription options to accommodate smaller budgets. NOZA is owned by Blackbaud.

Our favorite free search sites include the following:

- Bing (www.bing.com), DuckDuckGo (duckduckgo.com), and Google (www.google.com)

    These are our favorite search engines, but there are many more out there. Whatever search engine you choose, just make sure you learn how to use it well.

- Boat Info World (www.boatinfoworld.com) and Landings Airplane Ownership (www.landings.com)

    Both of these sites provide information about luxury goods, which can be an indication of wealth. They are searchable by owner name.

- CQ MoneyLine (http://cqmoneyline.com) and OpenSecrets (www.opensecrets.org)

    These sites allow you to search for federal election campaign contributions.

- U.S. Securities and Exchange Commission (www.sec.gov)

    If your prospect is a public company insider, you can find much that you need to know about his company holdings in SEC filings, but you will need to be able to understand these complicated financial documents.

- Pulawski Tax Assessor List (www.pulawski.net) and Zillow (www.zillow.com)

    Pulawski's website guides you to the tax assessor websites in each county in each state in the United States where you can search for a prospect's real estate holdings. Zillow gives you a fair estimate of a residential property's market value.

Analytics Tools

Analytics tools dig into your database or other data you have collected in an attempt to answer specific, strategic questions, such as "Who should receive our mail appeal this quarter?" or "How many people in our database have the capacity and are likely to give to our capital campaign at the various gift levels proposed?"

Analytics is most often used when we have a large group of donors and nondonors and want to find specific types of prospects. In the analytics field you may see terms including *data modeling*, *data mining*, *statistical analysis*, *regression models*, *scoring*, and *rating*. To learn more about using analytics to find prospects, read Chapter 2, Identifying New Prospects.

When we talk about using data analytics tools to help us to find prospects, we are referring to a sophisticated approach usually involving at least 5,000 database records and ideally 10,000 or more records. The most common data analytics project is to have a vendor evaluate an exported file from your database and deliver results to you in the form of "likelihood to give" ratings or other kinds of reporting. This is usually one piece of what might be called a "prospect screening" or "electronic screening."

TABLE 5.2   **Analytics Vendors**

Do it for you (fee)	Do it yourself (fee)	Do it yourself (free)
ADVIZOR Solutions (www.advizorsolutions.com)	DataDesk (www.datadesk.com)	Microsoft Excel R (www.r-project.org)
Blackbaud Target Analytics (www.blackbaud.com)	SAS (www.sas.com)	
DonorTrends (www.donortrends.com)	SPSS (www.o1.ibm.com/ software/analytics/spss/	
DonorScape (www.donorscape.com)		
Rapid Insight (www.rapidinsightinc.com)		
Reeher Group (www.reeher.net)		
WealthEngine (www.wealthengine.com)		

However, organizations with very large databases—hundreds of thousands of records—use analytics to change the way they fundraise and usually hire a specialized employee or consultant to help them. Higher education institutions might also recruit their own professors with specialized knowledge of statistics and/or hire an internal data analyst for the development department. Increasingly, membership organizations with large numbers of records in their database are also hiring internal analytics staff.

Table 5.2 identifies popular vendors. Although there is overlap between categories, we divided the list into three categories:

- Vendors best known for doing analytics projects, often in conjunction with other services like a wealth screening.
- Vendors popular for prospect research staff doing in-house projects.
- Vendors offering free software for analytics projects.

Summary Look-Up Tools

Summary look-up tools are often a marriage of analytics and search tools, giving you search options and ratings too. For example, in some software subscriptions, when you enter a name and other information such as home address, the software searches many databases and shows you a summary of what was found as well as giving you a suggested capacity rating. Some subscriptions also let you search the underlying databases independently.

CASE STUDY

Sharon, a director of development at a healthcare organization, purchased a wealth screening of her organization's 5,500 current donors to find prospects for a $2 million campaign for the clinic's expansion project. She received wealth detail reports on her name matches as well as capacity ratings for every name submitted. If no wealth match was found, the capacity rating was based on general demographic information.

Her organization's database manager then imported the capacity ratings. As part of the wealth screening package, Sharon's organization also received a one-year subscription to the look-up tool. Sharon used this to search for wealth information about prospects who were identified later by the campaign committee. The look-up tool showed her wealth results such as real estate owned, and gave her a capacity rating for each prospect.

Some popular look-up tools include:

- Blackbaud's ResearchPoint (www.blackbaud.com)
- DonorSearch (www.donorsearch.net)
- DonorScape (www.donorscape.com)
- WealthEngine (www.wealthengine.com)

Evaluating and Choosing a Tool

Choosing which tool or set of tools to use might seem overwhelming when there are so many vendors available. You might consider using something like the following process to evaluate and select a subscription:

- Write down your specific need.
- Conduct a general search online and at conference exhibit halls to narrow your choices and educate yourself on the possibilities.
- Ask colleagues about their experiences and ask for recommendations.
- Review your specific need again. Do you need to adjust anything?
- Contact two or three vendors and explain your needs.
- Prepare a test file or use a free demo. Be sure to include names of those you know well, those you do not know, and those you want to know. Be sure that the people who will be using the product have input.
- Review the results with each vendor.
- Ask for concurrent one-week trial subscriptions to each vendor's web-based look-up tool. For each tool, look up the same five entities that you know very well, five that you know something about, and five that you know nothing about. Which service was easiest to use? Which provided the information you needed in the format you preferred.
- Make a decision.
- Review your needs and vendors annually.

Other considerations when making a purchasing decision include the value you expect to receive and any training requirements. How many times will you be accessing the subscription? How will the research be used to raise more money? Is training necessary to get the most out of the subscription?

Once you purchase a subscription, be sure to review it annually. How often did users access the subscription? Do you have any additional needs since the subscription was purchased? Did the vendor add (or remove) sources or services?

OPTIONS FOR THE ONE-PERSON (OR SMALL-TEAM) DEVELOPMENT OFFICE

If you are the sole person working in the fundraising department or if you have a small development team, you may be wondering how you could possibly incorporate prospect research into your fundraising plan when it so often takes time and training to work well. Being aware of how prospect research can positively affect each stage of the development cycle will give you the foundation on which to seek resources and help when appropriate. Here are some real life examples where outsourcing and/or a combination of in-house expertise and outsourcing have led to success.

REAL LIFE EXAMPLES

ON TIME AND IN BUDGET, BY SUZANNE L. SEITER, CFRE, PRINCIPAL OF SOS CONSULTING

I was recruited as Vice President for Development to lead the campaign to build the National Constitution Center in Philadelphia. The goal was $77 million, including capital and endowment. I came on board with 14 months until the Center opened. As part of our fundraising strategy, we tackled prospect research in several cost-effective ways:

- **Personnel:** Although we could not afford a staff researcher, we did employ liberal arts undergrads from the University of Pennsylvania as interns during the summer and academic year. These students were eager, research-savvy, and totally comfortable searching the web for information on prospects. Fortunately, most of them were also good writers. The biggest challenge in supervising the work of the interns was in helping them understand what information we really needed and then how to distill large amounts of research into a one- to two-page prospect profile.

- **Online resources:** While a great deal of information is free on the Internet, there are also some excellent resources that charge a significant fee. We tackled this challenge in a couple of ways.

  For information on corporations (whether as prospective donors or as background information on individual prospects), we subscribed to Hoovers Online for one month at a time. We batched our corporate research needs and completed them all in the month of our subscription. Generally, we subscribed for only two to three months a year and got all the corporate data that we needed.

  For information from news, business, and legal sources, we needed an online subscription. First we discovered that they offered a reduced rate to nonprofits—but it was still quite expensive. We learned that several people on our board had the subscription in their offices. One permitted us to use his firm's subscription without charge, saving us several thousands of dollars.

- **Exceptions:** For prospects with the potential to make really large gifts, we did dedicate a portion of our budget for professional research services, knowing that good information was key to making the right ask—and that the return on the investment would be very good.

- **Outcomes:** We raised $20 million in two years from more than 10,000 donors, the doors of the National Constitution Center opened on time on July 4, 2003, and the bills were all paid!

USING PROSPECT RESEARCH TO MAKE CONNECTIONS, BY SUZANNE NIXON, DIRECTOR OF DEVELOPMENT, DEVEREUX FLORIDA

Prior to joining Noah's Light Foundation I was Director of Development at Devereux Florida. A large service provider, Devereux Florida drew the majority of our revenue from state and local funding sources and only began serious, systematic fundraising a few years ago. Despite this, we had an urgent need to build a wellness center

(Continued)

to serve developmentally disabled and behaviorally challenged children. With a young and small development team and a shallow donor base, we determined a traditional capital campaign wasn't going to work. Based on this, we decided to organize a capital campaign cabinet with a few key donors and community leaders, seeking a few large gifts and state and federal grants.

We asked this group to identify donors who they thought might have capacity and some interest in the project. We took this list and asked a research firm to provide full profiles on these individuals—because we didn't know them well and they weren't current donors to our organization. Normally I wouldn't have the research completed at the front end, but this helped us to learn enough about the prospects to create cultivation strategies based on their interests, connections to our active donors, and giving histories.

As an example, we learned that one identified prospect, who had never made a cash contribution to our organization, helped to organize the initial invitation from the then-Governor to us to provide services in the state. He had then stepped away from our organization to work on another project. Research showed that this prospective donor also appeared to make sustaining gifts (gifts to endowments, gifts of land, etc.) and he had business connections with two current key donors to us. Armed with this information, our current donors asked him to tour our facility, reminded him of his original involvement with us and asked him to joining the cabinet. He did so and has since made important connections to state legislators, and there were discussions about a pledge to form an operating endowment for the wellness center to sustain operations.

Prospect Research Saves the Tour! by Carol Butera, CFRE, Vice President, Development at Children First

We have a program staff person who is just really great with people. He was doing an off-site training when he was approached by a woman who specifically mentioned that she would like to get financially involved with our organization. He referred her to me and told me she was a bit unusual.

I invited her for our customary tour of the facilities. Before the day arrived. I went to Google and searched. Then I went to the county real estate website. The woman had significant capacity and was philanthropic! When she arrived for the tour she looked like the neighbor next door and throughout the tour she was very indifferent. A bit discouraged but armed with the knowledge that she was interested and capable, I continued the tour to the last room. That's when her eyes lit up and she was obviously interested in the program. Finally!

When I brought her into my office at the end of the tour, she said, "I know what I want to do." The bridge was crossed and we began discussing a gift. She made an initial gift of around $100,000 and continues to deepen her engagement with our organization.

If I had not known how to do that first round of research I might have given up on her early in the tour. Now, Children First has a generous new friend who is making a difference in children's lives.

Planned Giving Program + Donor Research = Success! by David Lepper, Senior Consultant with The Remington Group

Before I started consulting I was running a development shop and we had just started a planned-giving program. We sent out a postcard mailing. One of the recipients was a doctor who had made something like one small gift over 20 years—not your ideal prospect! He had made the list as the result of an age append to the database. But the postcard prompted his surviving life partner (he had died recently) to contact our school and he made a $100,000 gift. Nice, but not huge.

We did our homework on him and discovered that there were significant real-estate holdings. We now knew we had a significant major gift prospect. At one point while we were talking with him, he complained about real-estate taxes. I told him that we could help him with that. It was then that he volunteered the information about the real estate. In the end, he donated two homes worth $15 million and a building was named in his honor. He was very pleased with the gift—his partner had spoken well of the school and was grateful to it for his career—so pleased that, single and childless, he continued to give, making other significant gifts.

SUMMARY

Managing prospect research requires you to know how research helps you raise more money. From there you can make better decisions about hiring, training, and tools. It also means creating a feedback loop with your researcher. Whether the researcher is a vendor, consultant, or employee, communicating your request is not enough. You must also debrief after the information has been received so that future reports can meet your needs even better.

When it comes to assigning prospect research tasks, organizations take many different approaches. You can assign different tasks to multiple employees, hire a prospect researcher or intern, use volunteers or outsource. Whoever supervises prospect research needs to recognize that although prospect research is deeply interconnected with the database and technology, it is part of fundraising, and prospect research employees need to interact directly with frontline fundraisers, especially in the area of major gifts.

Prospect research is a specialized profession and can be highly technical. If your organization's prospect researcher does not receive training or is kept out of the loop of your fundraising projects, she will be handicapped and you will likely be disappointed with her results.

There are many free tools available for prospect researchers, but as your organization increases its demand for better information, you will find yourself shopping for fee-based subscriptions. Search engines only provide access to a small portion of what is available on the internet, and there is a world of information available off-line. As we discussed, there are three main types of research tools:

1. Search tools that help you find information about individuals, companies, and foundations.
2. Analytics tools that allow trained employees or consultants to manipulate a large number of records to find the best prospects for different initiatives and to better evaluate and measure fundraising efforts. These tools include vendors offering electronic screenings.
3. Summary look-up tools that combine analytics with search. The most common example is a wealth-screening package that includes

a look-up tool for searching one name at a time. The large group of records matched for wealth is returned to the organization, but a subscription to the look-up tool continues, usually for a year, and often includes a capacity rating or access to prospect identification resources.

As you are evaluating and choosing tools, you can take an organized approach to avoid being overwhelmed by your choices. The most important step is to first decide what you need to accomplish and then start shopping for solutions. As you become more educated about the offerings, you might find yourself adjusting your view of what you want to accomplish. Keep in mind that research tasks should always lead to improved fundraising performance. Before you buy, ask yourself the following: "Will this positively impact our fundraising bottom line?"

No matter what size operation you run or how many fundraising staff you employ, you can use effective prospect research strategies to reach your fundraising goals. Although large institutions dominate the conversation about prospect research, many small organizations successfully capitalize on the power of prospect research.

FOR FURTHER READING

APRA. "2012 Salary Survey Report." Chicago, IL: Smith Bucklin, October 2012.
Birkholz, Joshua. *Fundraising Analytics: Using Data to Guide Strategy*. Hoboken, NJ: John Wiley & Sons, 2008.
Strand, Bobbie J. *A Kaleidoscope of Prospect Development: The Shapes and Shades of Major Donor Prospecting*. Washington, DC: Council for Advancement and Support of Education (CASE), 2008.

CHAPTER **6**

Ethics, Risk, and Data Protection: What's the Big Deal?

If you spend any amount of time with a group of prospect researchers, you will notice that the topics of ethics and risk come up fairly frequently. Researchers work with sensitive information every day and are often the ones responsible for managing how confidential data gets stored in the database and files. Sometimes you may think that researchers are a little *too* concerned with ethics and risk, but you're about to learn why that's a good thing—how it can keep the trust of your donors and keep your organization out of legal hot water.

STARTING WITH DONOR TRUST

There have been a number of studies released within the past 10 years showing that public confidence in charitable organizations is eroding. In March 2008 a survey was done by Professor Paul Light, founding principal investigator at the Organizational Performance Initiative at New York University's Robert F. Wagner Graduate School of Public Service. Light's research found that the public's confidence in nonprofit organizations dropped sharply in the wake of September 11, 2001, when reports of charitable disbursements were scandal–ridden. By 2008 confidence had still not recovered to pre–2001 levels.

Light's survey showed that over one-third of Americans stated that they had very little confidence in charitable organizations and only 25 percent said charitable organizations were "very good" at helping people. In the survey, 70 percent of Americans said that charitable organizations waste "a great deal" or a "fair amount" of money, a figure that actually rose 10 percentage points from an earlier 2003 survey.

Poor public opinion is a pretty big hill to climb when you're trying to raise money, but there are other obstacles, some of them internal. Preventing harm and minimizing the impact of unavoidable harm are fundamental to both risk management and ethics, says Dr. Bruce Weinstein, author of *Ethical Intelligence: Five Principles for Untangling Your Toughest Problems at Work and Beyond*. But risk management and ethical behavior aren't exactly the same thing, so let's take a look at what they are and how they're different.

RISKY BUSINESS

Risk management is involved in preventing our organization and/or our donors from harm, and it's the "or" that separates risk from ethics. Risk management could place the nonprofit organization (rather than the donor) at the center of its priorities. Two examples are:

1. Prospect researchers at a college might conduct due diligence research on a corporation that the college is considering asking for a gift to name its science center. If the corporation is not a good corporate citizen, by accepting a donation from the company, the college could risk loss of its reputation, future funding and accreditation, or worse.
2. Let's say there is a case of long–term sexual misconduct by an individual at a university. The university's leadership might decide to handle it internally without alerting authorities, or ignore the evidence altogether to prevent the risk that the public might hear and donations might be affected.

In both of these cases, the nonprofit has placed itself rather than its donors or the constituency it serves as the center of risk avoidance, and the actions were intentional. But risky behavior can take all kinds of forms, some of it unintentional, lazy, or ignorant, including:

- Sloppy record keeping.
- Taking money from shady characters.
- Providing sweetheart real-estate deals to major donors.
- Using a charity's humanitarian relief jet to whisk the chief executive and family to their vacation destination.
- Allowing donors' credit card numbers to sit out on a desk overnight.
- Leaving a donor file or laptop in the back seat of a taxi.
- Throwing information in the trash that should be shredded.

Prospect researchers are primarily involved in risk management where the gathering and recording of donor data is involved. Let's take a look at how ethics come into play.

<table>
<tr><td>CASE STUDY</td><td>A SCHOOL OF PUBLIC HEALTH DISCOVERS A NEED FOR AN ETHICS STATEMENT</td></tr>
</table>

Several years ago, the dean of Bronilla University School of Public Health was approached by a national corporation that wanted to make a large donation in support of the school's community-based violence prevention and research program. The donation was significant; in fact, it would have been nearly half of the program's operating budget for five years. The company had a track record of generous and continuing philanthropy to organizations it supported, but what troubled the dean was their product: handguns. The dean brought the offer for consideration to the school's governing board. The board decided unanimously to thank the company, but

(Continued)

to decline the donation. A special retreat was convened a few months later where the board and senior staff crafted the school's first ethics statement, providing leadership with guidelines for accepting (or rejecting) philanthropic support from companies manufacturing or selling goods that were in conflict with its mission.

ETHICS

Ethics is related to risk, but where risk is affected by external factors, ethics are internal—to each individual and within an organizational culture. As Lilya Wagner, director of Philanthropic Service for Institutions at the North America Division of the Seventh-Day Adventist Church, writes,

> *Ethics aren't simply a list of behaviors, a set of restrictions on what we can and cannot do. Ethics aren't just something we do because we know people are watching us. Ethics are a reflection of ourselves. Ethical behavior expresses who we are, what values we hold dear and what principles we will always fight for. Our ethics go straight to the heart of who we are.*

Ethics are agreed-upon values or a policy statement. One example is a mental health organization that promises not to publish its list of donors because sharing that information might be embarrassing to donors. Another example might be a research center that declines a gift because the donor expected special treatment or a quid pro quo.

Prospect researchers that are members of the Association of Professional Researchers for Advancement (APRA) are required to sign an agreement affirming their intention to abide by the Association's Statement of Ethics. This Statement is available in the appendix of this book, and also online at the APRA website (www.aprahome.org). To keep abreast of changing laws and professional standards, APRA's Statement of Ethics has been revised several times over the years, most recently in 2009.

Many nonprofit organizations opt to create their own code of ethics that employees agree to follow. Some go further with a written policy statement designed to mitigate the possibility of damage or to legally protect the organization from purposefully risky behavior.

Does your organization have its own code of ethics? What are its policies to reduce exposure and manage risk? Ask your supervisor or your organization's lawyer (or legal department) if you are not sure. Consider creating your own policies using the resources here and online as a guide.

LEGAL ISSUES

As mentioned previously, researchers are often the ones charged with managing how confidential data gets stored in the database, and this takes ethics and risk one step further—into the realm of legal requirements. While an ethics statement and risk mitigation policy may be important to have, they're not generally legally binding. Data protection laws *are* binding, though, and it's critically important for you, your research team, and anyone who has access to data in your system to be aware of and abide by state and federal laws that cover your organization's data management and privacy protection.

Data protection laws are very different from one country to the next, from one organization type to another, and sometimes even from one U.S. state to its neighbor. Many organizations require new employees to undergo training to understand how these laws impact their work. If yours does not, we strongly recommend that you take the time to find out how you and your organization need to comply. Here is a sampling of the regulations that may relate to your organization.

The Family Educational Rights and Privacy Act (FERPA), also referred to as the Buckley Amendment, is a U.S. federal law enacted in 1974 and revised most recently in 2008 to protect the privacy of a student's school records. It impacts all educational institutions that receive federal funding. FERPA broadly stipulates that:

- Parents have the right of access to their child's records until the student turns 18 (when the rights transfer to the student).

- A school must correct any information within the student's record that is incorrect or misleading.
- Written permission from a parent or student must be obtained before certain pieces of information may be shared with outside parties, with several exceptions.

FERPA allows sharing of "directory" information "such as a student's name, address, telephone number, date and place of birth, honors and awards, and dates of attendance. However, schools must tell parents and eligible students about directory information and allow parents and eligible students a reasonable amount of time to request that the school not disclose directory information about them."[1] That can include an annual letter as well as a page on the school's or university's website informing the community about data handling policies.

The Health Insurance Portability and Accountability Act of 1996 (HIPAA), also sometimes referred to as the Privacy Rule, was written to protect individuals from their personal health-related information being shared without their consent. It impacts all health plans, healthcare providers and healthcare clearinghouses in the United States, from major research medical centers and community hospitals to local dentist offices, acupuncturists, and health spas. The Privacy Rule protects all "individually identifiable health information" held or transmitted by an organization or its business associates in any form. The Privacy Rule calls this information "protected health information" or PHI.[2] According to the law, "Individually identifiable health information" is information, including demographic data:

- That relates to the individual's past, present, or future physical or mental health or condition.

---

[1] "Family Education Rights and Privacy Act (FERPA)," U.S. Department of Education, www2.ed.gov/policy/gen/guid/fpco/ferpa/index.html.

[2] "Summary of the HIPAA Privacy Rule," U.S. Department of Health and Human Services, www.hhs.gov/ocr/privacy/hipaa/understanding/summary/index.html.

- That relates to the provision of healthcare to the individual, or the past, present, or future payment for the provision of healthcare to the individual.
- That identifies the individual or for which there is a reasonable basis to believe it can be used to identify the individual. Individually identifiable health information includes many common identifiers (e.g., name, address, birth date, and Social Security number).

While that sounds completely exclusionary to fundraising, the HIPAA laws were recently clarified to include fundraising offices as entities that admissions could share certain information with.

AVOIDING RISK: NEW LAWS IMPACT NONPROFITS AND INCREASE HEADLINES

Since August 2009, risk avoidance has taken on new meaning for healthcare organizations. Congress ruled that if a healthcare organization discovers a data breach involving more than 500 records, the organization must not only notify the Department of Health and Human Services of the breach *but must also inform the media*.

OUTSIDE OF THE UNITED STATES

United Kingdom

In the United Kingdom, the law by which all organizations—both business and charitable—must abide is the Data Protection Act of 1998. Complete details of the Act and how it applies (and should be applied) is available at the Information Commissioner's Office.

The Act covers an organization's internal handling of their clients' or constituency's personal information, the way the information is transmitted manually or electronically to another entity, the way that an organization may use the personal data to contact their constituents, and an organization's legal obligation to make some information public.

The website of the Institute of Fundraising (IOF) has a very helpful page on data protection and compliance, and Researchers in Fundraising, a special interest group of the IOF, has put together a white paper specific to prospect research and data compliance in the United Kingdom. Links to both online sources can be found at the end of this chapter.

Canada

In Canada there are two laws that govern data protection, the Privacy Act and the Personal Information Protection and Electronic Documents Act (PIPEDA), which was implemented in three stages between January 2001 and January 2004. PIPEDA applies to any non–governmental organization and relates to any personal information gathered during the course of business.

The provinces of British Columbia, Alberta, and Quebec have passed privacy laws similar to PIPEDA, and Ontario has adopted laws relevant to the collection of personal health information. Because they are substantially similar, the Canadian government determined that a charity was obligated to abide by its province's laws governing privacy and data handling. The Association of Fundraising Professionals (AFP), in collaboration with the Association for Healthcare Philanthropy (AHP), APRA, and Imagine Canada (formerly the Canadian Centre for Philanthropy) jointly published a white paper designed to help fundraisers comply with Canadian laws. More information about how to locate this document can be found at the end of this chapter.

SOME PRACTICAL TIPS

Some practical tips for protecting donor information include:

- Unless you still need it or must file it, shred every piece of paper that has a name or a number on it. This simple rule may seem overly broad, but it's easy to remember and gives you maximum risk protection.
- Never send donor information (attached documents, spreadsheets, etc.) via e-mail, even internally, unless it's encrypted and/or password protected. Use a secure server and FTP when possible.

- Never leave donor information, including files, gift receipts, or even proposals, sitting out on your desk overnight. Put papers you are still working on in a locked drawer in your desk; you never know who has access to your office after you leave it.
- Maintain strict security protocols for your database and limit who has access to it. Change passwords frequently. Be sure that former employees no longer have access to data.
- Create a confidentiality agreement ensuring that new employees know your organization's risk and confidentiality policies. Enact protocols to prevent former employees from taking confidential lists or donor information with them when they leave.
- Never allow donor files, research, or other confidential information to leave the office except under very controlled situations (sharing with your president or board chair, for example). Impress upon top volunteers the importance of properly maintaining the security of these documents: Your care on this issue will assure them that you are doing the same with information about them.
- Be aware of the laws that govern your organization type and ensure they are enforced.

SUMMARY

Ethics and risk guidelines aren't just fuzzy feel-good notions to uphold; they protect you, your board, your organization, and your donors from real harm. Professional associations for frontline fundraisers and prospect researchers such as AFP, AHP, and APRA keep current on guidelines as they evolve, and are great resources if you have questions or concerns about your organization and compliance.

FOR FURTHER READING

AFP. "AFP Ethics Assessment Inventory." www.afpnet.org/Audiences/Member NewsDetail.cfm?ItemNumber=5754.

AFP. "Privacy 101: A Guide to Privacy Legislation for Fundraising Professionals in Canada." www.afpnet.org/Audiences/PublicolicyIssueDetail.cfm?Item Number=1053.

AFP, AHP, APRA, and Imagine Canada. "Fundraising and Privacy: Complying with Federal and Provincial Laws." www.afpnet.org/files/ContentDocuments /canada_privacy_guidance_document_jan_2004.pdf

AHP. "Fundraising Under HIPAA: An AHP Research to Practice Guide." www .ahp.org/publicationandtools/bookstore/Pages/HIPAAGuide.aspx.

Information Commissioner's Office. "Data Protection Act: Your Responsibilities and Obligations to Data Protection." www.ico.gov.uk/for_organisations/ data_protection.aspx.

Institute of Fundraising. "Data Protection." www.institute-of-fundraising.org.uk/ guidance/about-fundraising/data-protection/.

Office of the Privacy Commissioner of Canada. Resources. www.priv.gc.ca/ information/index_e.asp

Researchers in Fundraising. "Data Protection Guidelines." IOF. www.institute-of-fundraising.org.uk/groups/sig-researchers/rif-publications/.

Schultz, David. "As Patients' Records Go Digital, Theft and Hacking Problems Grow." *Kaiser Health News*, June 3, 2012. www.kaiserhealthnews.org/ Stories/2012/June/04/electronic-health-records-theft-hacking.aspx.

CHAPTER 7

International Prospect Research

The big trend in continental Europe is prospect research itself. Because fundraising in most organisations has been either focused on government funding or on direct marketing, there has been no need to develop a prospect research function. Today, thanks to encouragement from colleagues in other countries and in part from the pressure caused by severe and sudden reductions in government spending, non-profits are beginning to create prospect research functions as part of a "major donor" team.

Organisations such as INSEAD and HEC in France, and Médecins Sans Frontières in Spain and the Netherlands, have been leading the way with prospect research.

—CHRIS CARNIE, Factary Europe

D onors from Europe and emerging markets like China and India are becoming ever more familiar faces in the world of large, philanthropic giving. Wealthy individuals around the globe have begun participating in significant philanthropic giving in their home countries and abroad. Many fundraisers here in the United States have been taking notice of the trend, and even some small organizations are beginning to seek gifts from international donors. Large institutions of higher education were among the first to step into the arena, but all types of organizations are beginning to find international prospects in their midst as global wealth increases.

In this chapter we will share stories about how other organizations have been successful fundraising outside of the United States, and we will discuss how international prospect research differs from the traditional approaches in the United States.

MAKING INTERNATIONAL FUNDRAISING WORK

International is a very big word. It encompasses a vast array of languages, cultures, geography, and more. As big as it is, there are organizations managing relationships and raising significant gifts in countries around the world. You may be one of those organizations, or you may be mystified about how international fundraising works. We have interviewed people from three organizations that are successfully making it happen. Each of these stories demonstrates how important prospect research is and the similarities and differences between international fundraising and the traditional U.S. approach.

Back to Fundamentals with Habitat for Humanity

Habitat for Humanity (www.habitat.org) raises $100 million a year outside of the United States. They employ several dozen relationship fundraisers in four continents. How do they do it? John P. Cerniglia, CFRE, Senior Director was kind enough to share an example.

In preparation for his visit to Jakarta in Indonesia, he asked Habitat's prospect researcher to pull a list of the top 100 Indonesians. He reviewed the list and narrowed it down to 10 that seemed the most likely to be interested in Habitat for Humanity and connected to people in the community. In Jakarta, he sat down with his campaign cabinet chair and they reviewed the list. The campaign cabinet chair immediately recognized people on the list and had close relationships with some. For example, he and one of the prospects regularly went skiing together in the United States. After identifying individuals with which the organization had a connection, John began working with the campaign cabinet chair to create a strategy for introducing those individuals to Habitat for Humanity.

Prospect research was helpful as John set out for Jakarta, but recruiting local volunteer leaders who were social peers of the very wealthy was key. In many countries, those with wealth are much wealthier than others in their community; there is little or no middle class. Within a small community of very wealthy people like this, networking to identify and create linkages to your organization is more important than traditional "desktop" prospect research.

A Certified Fundraising Executive (CFRE), John was quick to point out that the fundamentals of relationship fundraising apply equally to international prospects. Before spending resources, he and his colleagues establish if a prospect has linkage, ability, and inclination. He emphasized that linkage, colorfully described as "psychic debt," is the first and most important step with a prospect. If a prospect does not feel closely aligned with an organization, a substantial gift is much less likely. He also suggested that just because a prospect is sending his child to a private U.S. school or a camp in Canada, this does not automatically suggest great wealth. The family may be stretching its resources to invest in the future of its next generation.

The search for evidence of philanthropic giving should also not be skipped. One of John's strategies when looking for the best possible international prospects is to focus on those who have already made a gift in the United States, often to a higher education institution. He finds that a prospect who has already been introduced to Western-style philanthropy is easier to cultivate.

Although John advocates the fundraising fundamentals, he notes that the big difference in international fundraising is that you must match the cultivation and solicitation approach to the culture in which you are operating. This should vary wildly depending upon the country.

John's advice to fundraisers is that they should not be chasing cold prospects—domestic or international. If the linkage to an international prospect is weak, time would be better spent finding warmer prospects.

Wycliffe Courts Asian-American Donors

Jeff Lee has been an Asian-American fundraiser for more than 15 years. Currently he serves as International Philanthropy Director for Wycliffe Bible Translators (www.wycliffe.org). Soon after he joined Wycliffe, the organization's Philippines office asked him for help with its major-gifts initiative. Eight months later they solicited a prospect for a gift of $1 million in U.S. dollars!

Like Habitat for Humanity, Wycliffe has operations all over the world and has been cultivating many small communities of very wealthy individuals. Jeff was able to help the Philippines office create a compelling case for support, identify projects with appeal to donors, and create a strategy to ask for each gift. He said that Wycliffe frequently networks through the churches, which may be the focal point of a community. In this way, the company attracts top business people to their local boards. These people have social relationships with other wealthy individuals in the community, and as business leaders, they quickly grasp fundraising strategy.

In 1999, Wycliffe embarked on its Last Languages Campaign (www.lastlanguagescampaign.org). The goal of this campaign is to see a Bible translation program started in every language still needing one by the year 2025. In Asia, Wycliffe is involved in 418 projects. Jeff is part of the effort to train and empower Wycliffe's partner agencies in Asia to raise major gifts and practice sustainable fundraising strategies. He is energized and excited by the opportunities there.

Asia is predicted to be the wealthiest place on the globe by 2025. Based in California, Jeff sits in the state with the largest Asian-American community. Jeff focuses primarily on cultivating people in the Chinese and Korean communities. He finds that Asian migrants from mainland China have been settling in the United States, with or without their wives, and are sending their children to school here. By cultivating Asian Americans throughout the United States, Jeff hopes to position Wycliffe as a connecting point between the Asian community in the United States and in Asia.

Originally, Wycliffe's talented group of prospect researchers wanted to send him prospects from the donor database, but Jeff found that these were not leading him to the wealthiest of the Asian-American community. Instead, Jeff has been identifying high-net-worth individuals through churches and other groups. His many years of fundraising in the Asian-American community have allowed him to quickly recognize good prospects and to make new connections. Once he has identified a prospect, he calls upon the prospect research staff for more information, and this has been helpful in creating cultivation strategies.

Jeff's method of reaching out into the community with a clear case for support and of leveraging a wealthy social network to reach prospects is sound fundraising strategy. His challenge is to deepen donors' relationship with Wycliffe enough to create a network that connects and leverages relationships and resources between the United States and Asia.

Coordinating Information at Rotary International

The Rotary Foundation (www.rotary.org) is the philanthropic arm of Rotary International, an organization supporting clubs in more than 200 countries around the globe. Sabine Schuller is the sole prospect researcher, working with around 40 frontline fundraisers and a foundation with a global reach. Because The Rotary Foundation is a membership organization, it primarily looks to its members for donations. Like most researchers, Sabine seeks to combine first-hand information from the prospect, secondhand information from peers, and thirdhand information found online and off-line through anonymous searches.

Firsthand Information Just as she does for U.S. prospects, Sabine must record and use information given by the donor prospect directly.

Rotary provides rich opportunities for members to share information about themselves, including membership forms and awards, and it has archives of information on members to draw from.

Secondhand Information   This is where Rotary really shines. Because there are Rotary clubs around the world, Sabine and her co-workers are able to call upon local Rotarians in other countries to find people who know her prospect. This way she can learn important things like whether someone plans to sell her business soon or the names of close family members involved in a gift. This kind of information takes longer to collect, but is much more rich, especially in countries were high-net-worth social circles are small.

Thirdhand Information   Sabine has located some great subscription databases for online searching for different countries. Some of them she subscribes to, and some of them are cost prohibitive. She uses online searching when she can and when it makes the most sense for a given prospect.

Strength in Stewardship   Rotary's structure is such that in addition to paid gift officers, there are volunteers whose roles include soliciting and stewarding donors. Senior leadership often travels internationally and will visit donors informally to thank them. In some countries, the Rotary Foundation has Associate Foundations to facilitate giving. Through these activities Rotary combines Western-style philanthropy with a local approach.

In support of these activities, Sabine's focus is on pulling the relevant information together from all of the different places Rotary collects it, finding and adding missing information, and delivering it to the right people. Sabine enjoys the change of pace and challenges that come with researching international prospects—especially when a golden nugget of information is found on an old-fashioned index card filed away deep in the archives!

Getting Started with International Prospects

Your organization might have a sprinkling of international prospects, might want to better identify and approach international prospects, or might have other plans and ideas on international fundraising. A prospect researcher can do more than prepare profiles for you; he can help you find wealth reports and help answer questions about the country that will inform your strategy.

> *Use your professional network to talk with peers who have had success with international prospects. I have yet to come across a fundraiser who would not share with me.*

> —John P. Cerniglia, CFRE, Senior Director of Habitat for Humanity International

Evaluate and Rate

Although you might rely mostly on prospect research to evaluate and rate your U.S. prospects, international prospects may require more direct contact or peer discussions to determine if there is a connection and interest in your organization. Without a link or connection, an international prospect is a cold and expensive prospect. Once you have established a connection, even the question of ability to give, and giving history, might best be answered by the donor prospect and her peers, with online searching as a complement.

Sources of Information

International prospect research is not impossible to do, but the information available on individuals and companies outside of the United States and the United Kingdom is scarce, difficult to find and limited. As demonstrated by the previous case studies, your best source of information on international prospects is likely to be the prospects themselves or someone who knows them well.

In the United States and United Kingdom we are fortunate to have access to a number of free and fee-based resources that provide us with a good deal of information on prospective donors. Researching entities in the United Kingdom is also relatively straightforward, as the cultural bias toward access to information is generally the same to that in the United States. You may be expected to pay for access, but the data is—for the most part—similarly available.

As wealth and philanthropy grow around the world, the information landscape is likely to shift. Business has long been interested in global information, and there are reports, periodicals, blogs, and other sources that provide detailed information about specific countries, including business, wealth, and philanthropy. In the United States there are a growing number of prospect researchers specializing in international research. As you plan your international approach you will want to look for the following:

- People in your professional network who are successful with international fundraising, especially in the country where you will focus your efforts.
- The best free and/or fee sources of news and cultural information.
- Finding or developing expertise in researching wealth and giving in the country where you will focus.

Visit the companion website to this book at www.Research4 Fundraisers.com to find online resources that may be helpful to you.

Tax Laws

Another consideration as you approach international prospects is how attractive your organization is from a tax perspective. Unless an international charity has a U.S.-based 501(c)(3), U.S. donors may think twice about giving to a foreign entity. Especially when structuring a major gift, many donors consider tax advantages as part of their gift planning. It is the same for donors outside of the United States who may want to give to a nonprofit here. International tax laws do not make giving to U.S.-based charities attractive, and some countries provide a negative incentive to give outside of their country.

- Does your organization provide access for donors to make tax-efficient gifts to your organization?
- Do you have prospective donors living abroad that also have residences or businesses in the United States? They may find a charitable donation attractive from a tax perspective.

SUMMARY

World economies are interdependent, many businesses operate on a global scale, and increasingly philanthropists are following that pattern when they consider making large-scale donations. Wealth and philanthropy are growing around the world and some U.S. organizations have been raising funds successfully overseas for years. Fundraising abroad follows many of the same fundamentals as in the United States. You must evaluate and rate your prospects, establishing some kind of linkage or connection to your cause, in order to make best use of your time and resources. A cold prospect is very expensive if there are warmer people with equal or greater philanthropic potential in your prospect pool.

When it comes to prospect research, international fundraising typically relies heavily on learning information directly from the prospect and her peers in the local community. Anonymous, online searching frequently takes a back seat to first- and secondhand information, and researchers may be asked to answer more generic questions about a country, its philanthropic customs, and its local communities.

Fundraisers hoping to be successful in international fundraising will want to become familiar with the news, cultural climate, and other relevant characteristics of the country they will be visiting. Look to your professional network to find others who have been successful with international donors or who are located in the country you will be visiting.

Visit the online companion to this book at www.Research4 Fundraisers.com to find resources for international prospecting and fundraising.

FOR FURTHER READING

Bandy, Beth. *International Fundraising Intelligence* blog. www.ifintelligence.com/ blog/.

Carnie, Christopher, and Cynthia W. Gentry. *Fundraising from Europe.* Lingfield: Chapel & York, 2003.

Harris, Thomas. *International Fund Raising for Not-for-Profits: A Country by Country Profile.* New York: John Wiley & Sons, 1999.

Koele, Ineke Alien. *International Taxation of Philanthropy: Removing Tax Obstacles for International Charities.* Amsterdam: IBFD Publications, 2007.

MacDonald, Norine, QC, and Tayart de Borms, Luc, eds. *Global Philanthropy.* Foreword by Stephan Schmidheiny. London: MF Publishing Ltd, 2010.

MacDonald, Norine, QC, and Tayart de Borms, Luc, eds. *Philanthropy in Europe. A Rich Past, a Promising Future.* London: Alliance Publishing Trust, 2008.

Norton, Michael. *The Worldwide Fundraiser's Handbook.* London: Directory of Social Change, 2003.

CHAPTER 8

Trends and Opportunities: The Future of Prospect Research

Prospect research has undergone tremendous changes over the past ten years. The need for information on our best donors and potential donors will never go away, but the ways prospect researchers provide information and contribute to an organization's fundraising success is going to continue to evolve in ways we can't begin to guess.

What is clear is that prospect research is changing rapidly, away from simply finding and providing information toward interpreting, analyzing and presenting information in ways that lead to new discoveries and help keep staff on track with performance and other benchmarks. In this chapter we cover a few of the trends most visible today, including the following:

- Big data and segmentation.
- Data visualization software applications.
- Relationship mapping.
- Social media and social scoring.
- Content curation.

All of these trends and opportunities are related to one another and to the common theme throughout this book: data. Translating data into donors is the goal of prospect research.

BIG DATA AND SEGMENTATION

In the world of information, big data is a collection of data that is so large and so complicated that our usual database tools are unable to cope with it, and it's been around for years now. Let's start with some examples you probably already know that illustrate the desired outcomes when big data is tamed.

Amazon.com made headlines when it began successfully harnessing the huge amount of data generated from traffic and purchase behavior on its website. As a shopper, you are fed popular purchase choices based on your browsing. When you make a purchase, you are given the opportunity to buy additional books that other people who have made the same purchase have also bought. You know the end of this story. Amazon has done a great job of selling a vast array of items on its website. The company was able to take huge amounts of data and make something meaningful—more sales—come out of analyzing and acting on it.

Another example is one of the most popular search engines, Google. Billions of searches every day creates a lot of data! One of Google's projects has been to analyze searching behavior data to try to predict trends in influenza epidemics. Google Flu Trends (www.google.org/flutrends) looks at things such as how many people are searching for information relating to diagnosing and treating the flu and tries to predict where there will be outbreaks. So far, their predictions have correlated well with actual outbreaks.

In the world of fundraising, big data might look like your usual donor database, but layered with individuals' click-throughs on your website, participation on your Twitter page, visits to your blog, or activity in related Facebook groups. You might also receive regular data files from sales of license plates, cause-related marketing or other fundraising efforts. Being able to hone in on your best prospects and move them to act and give has always been a challenge. The bigger the data, the richer your opportunity to learn about your constituency.

During the presidential campaign of 2008, Barack Obama's fundraising machine became legendary for its skill in using social media and market segmentation for more targeted approaches to donors. One of the things the campaign staff did was use e-mail click-throughs to determine a prospect's interest in a variety of topics. The first few, mostly general e-mails from the candidate, might include stories in three interest areas: the economy, healthcare, and the environment. If an individual consistently clicked only on stories in the economy section, future e-mails would be more heavily weighted to information about economic policy.

According to anecdotal research by Kivi Leroux Miller,[1] many nonprofit organizations still struggle to interact with donors who give online, often persistently sending them snail mail because that is the only way the organization communicates—all of their donors are in one segment. What Amazon, Google, and the Obama campaign have demonstrated is prowess at segmenting. Segmenting means that you separate your donors into groups based on specific characteristics. For example, people who prefer to make gifts online are sent e-mail communications, while those give offline are sent snail mail. The real power and challenge of segmentation becomes apparent as the underlying dataset grows.

Big-data and segmentation strategies are a growing trend that is likely to continue to become more accessible to organizations of every size. As big business and very large nonprofit organizations keep using and refining the techniques, new and easier-to-use software products will be created. Already donor database software has evolved into a more intuitive platform for evaluating fundraising performance. Software such as DonorPerfect, which reaches out to the smaller nonprofit organizations, has built-in reports that use basic best practices to evaluate

---

[1]Kivi Leroux Miller, "No Wonder Retention of Online Donors Is So Bad," *Kivi's Nonprofit Communications Blog*, August 21, 2012, accessed October 25, 2012, www.nonprofitmarketingguide.com.

annual fund performance. Your staff can instantly do some simple evaluation by using these reports. Especially because these software programs reside online in the cloud where upgrades are often automatic, we expect that sometime in the near future organizations will see more built-in segmentation and analytics tools become standard.

DATA VISUALIZATION

Imagine for a moment that when you, the frontline fundraiser, start your computer in the morning, a dashboard appears. This dashboard maps out your personal progress toward short- and long-term goals as well as your department or team's progress and shows the information in colorful charts and graphs to give you a quick snapshot. You can drill down on any graph to get the level of detail you want on any donor or project.

This is one type of data visualization, and some organizations are already using it. Visual reports can be created to track any metric that your organization collects in its database, including, but by no means limited to the following:

- Number of prospects identified, in cultivation, or previously solicited.
- Donors by geography, class, or member level.
- Revenue by city, state, industry, or class year.
- Proposals delivered, outstanding, accepted, or rejected.
- Most/least active fundraisers by number of visits or proposals sent.
- Fundraiser performance compared to peers.
- Cumulative activity by department or division.
- Anything the data in your database describes!

Although data visualization tools are being used by mostly large organizations right now, Salesforce is a good example of how these kinds of sophisticated tools are trickling down to smaller organizations. Salesforce began as an online business customer relationship management software service. As it has grown and expanded its services, it has reached out to offer database solutions to nonprofits. A colorful dashboard with bar charts and other graphic visualizations of important metrics is part of the program.

Another kind of data visualization is still in the realm of the very large and complex data sets most often found at large universities and hospitals. Software solutions offered by companies like ADVIZOR Solutions, Rapid Insight and the Reeher Group make data manipulation look very simple. Discovering new information about your donors and friends and creating careful groups and lists still requires a trained researcher who understands your data, but once some reports are created, other staff can fairly easily learn to use and manipulate some of the data themselves. Adding and moving criteria, such as dates or school affiliation, is a click-and-drag operation and the information is presented visually so it's easy to spot trends quickly.

This kind of data segmentation and analytics software still makes the most sense for very large organizations trying to slice and dice large data sets for a myriad of uses. A large university with multiple schools, sports teams, clubs, and other groups who are involved in fundraising and alumni relations have complex needs. The types of visual solutions available now have begun to change their requests for lists and data from one of "ask, wait, and receive" into more of a self-service option. The researcher can create the functionality for a school or division, and the person in that school or division can access and manipulate the data on demand.

Both types of data visualization applications make it easier for information to tell its story. Graphic dashboards can keep you and your organization on track to goals and objectives. Data manipulation applications can help you discover new things about the people and information in your data. Both types of applications make the information easier for the end user to understand and utilize.

RELATIONSHIP MAPPING

Relationship maps usually start with one donor or constituent at the center. A map is drawn with every known relationship between that entity and others such as business colleagues, fellow board members, family members, nonprofit and for-profit entities, social clubs, and such. The purpose of relationship maps is to find a connection between an organization, its close volunteers, and others that they may know who can make introductions to new prospects.

Relationship mapping in prospect research really isn't new, but it has yet to be done well as a provided service. Mapping is available as a module in some fundraising software programs and as an online service both free or with a fee from information vendors such as Factary and Market Visual. Relationship maps can be depicted graphically or in list format. Good relationship maps show:

- One individual's relationship to another individual (and/or organization).
- The strength and length of their relationship.
- The degree to which either individual has influence on the other.

To create maps yourself, start with your trustees, well-connected volunteers, influential members of your constituency, and long-time staff—anyone who would be willing and able to introduce you to others. Don't waste time mapping individuals that have told you that they are uncomfortable helping you make connections.

Here are the pieces of information you will want for the constituents you have selected.

- Current and former boards they've sat on, with dates of service.
- Others who have served on those boards at the same time.
- Family relationships and the boards those family members have served on, with dates.
- Any close classmates.
- Friends with whom they socialize.
- Fellow social club or civic members.
- Neighbors.
- Influential members at their place of worship.

Building data for relationship maps is an ongoing process. You don't need to have every single piece of data for the exercise to be helpful, but the more information you have, the stronger this resource will be for you. Don't waste time with six degrees of separation—once you get beyond two degrees the ties are too tenuous for you to build meaningful relationships.

HOW ONE COLLEGE USED LINKEDIN TO IDENTIFY PROSPECTIVE DONORS

With a donor base in the hundreds of thousands, a university in the Northeast wanted to find an innovative and efficient way to discover accurate information about the capacity of potential donors to give.

Working with marketing consultant Bruce Segal of ESQ Unlimited, they asked the question: "How do we identify which active donors have potential to increase their contribution and which are at risk of decreasing it?" With this information, the school could better evaluate the total amount it could raise in its campaign and determine the number of gifts it needed at specific dollar amounts—in other words, how to create its donor pyramid. The school also wanted to find well-connected alumni to involve in peer screenings.

Using data analytics, they found that an individual's influence in social circles was a good marker of their ability and likelihood to make a major gift to the school. These well-connected individuals also knew who felt close to the school or to their classmates, who started a new business or lost a job, and who were focused on finance-affecting issues like a job loss. The "Connectors" were more likely to know who in the alumni body was open to being approached and who was not.

The school had created a LinkedIn group and Segal developed a process to build lists of alumni who had the highest number of connections within that LinkedIn group. Next, they developed a process to subsegment the highly connected alumni into those who felt an affinity for the institution, and those who did not.

(Continued)

In the process, they discovered alumni the school didn't know felt close affinity to their alma mater; the individuals were well connected through their network of classmates but had been inactive through the alumni association or as donors.

In a short time, the school found a select group of alumni most likely to know others who could make connections for them, and identified individuals with potential for further involvement.

Relationship mapping is another powerful tool to help you identify great prospects you can then actively engage in your organization. The technique has been around a long time, but the software tools to collect relationship information, add external information to your relationship maps, and help you present a visual picture have been continually improving. Relationship mapping is not yet the magic wand that automatically populates relationships to your donors and friends, but expect it to get better and more intuitive in the future.

SOCIAL MEDIA AND SOCIAL SCORING

Although social networks such as Facebook, LinkedIn, YouTube, Twitter, Klout, and Google+ aren't new, how nonprofits are beginning to use them to research and interact with donors is a growing trend.

Mark Schaefer, a marketing and social media expert and the author of *Return on Influence: The Revolutionary Power of Klout, Social Scoring, and Influence Marketing* says:

> *Social media provides us with a huge opportunity to create human connections between a cause and its constituents. We have never had a better way to create and distribute content at such low cost, and for nonprofits that puts them even with brands like Coca-Cola or Johnson*

& Johnson, and with each other. Small nonprofits can compete on the same level playing fields as huge nonprofits, because it's so easy to connect and tell your story directly to people who are passionate about your mission.

Social scoring is a new social media tool that tracks an individual's influence in the social media sphere. In case you haven't heard of social scoring, it works like this: Companies like Klout, PeerIndex, and Kred look at the ways people interact with each other on social media. People whose tweets are reshared frequently, whose videos or blog posts go viral, or who can motivate people into some form of social-media or real-life action gain credibility points. The higher one's score, the more influence they are perceived to have. As people gain higher scores, they are categorized as being influential on specific topics. Companies have started mining that information to identify people who are scored as influencers and reward them with perks, such as test driving a luxury car for a week or a free hotel upgrade, in hopes that they will become brand advocates.

Could social scoring be used by nonprofits to identify potential brand advocates and donor prospects? Schaefer says:

Absolutely! Let's say you're ABC Nonprofit using a free service like HootSuite to monitor your social media accounts. You would create and save a search for ABC Nonprofit and start monitoring all of the tweets that mention ABC. You'll start to notice some of the same accounts mentioning you, and you can cherry-pick them one by one to identify prospects. Or you can filter that stream by Klout score to only see those with an influence score of 50 or above.

Schaefer suggests that you could now use the prospect list to invite high-level influencers to insiders-only events. If the individuals have a good time, it's likely they'll tweet about your nonprofit even more. Companies like Radian6, Appinions, and Orgnet are devising strategies to help organizations identify potential donors and volunteers with influence, affluence, and well-connected networks. With this kind of approach, you could conceivably identify potential board members, volunteers, or major-gift prospects among your social media influencers.

It's a brave new world, but it's not for everyone.

Debates are ongoing within the prospect research community about the ethical uses of these forms of direct access to information about prospects. In addition, it's always smart to be aware of the terms and conditions and privacy policies for each network that govern the collection and storage of information from these sources. Privacy policies change frequently and many end users aren't aware of the extent to which personal information is available for anyone to see. Just as with all other forms of information gathering, it's both smart and legally responsible to have a clear policy for the ways you handle data for your entire fundraising operation, not just for prospect research.

Also, it doesn't make sense to spend a lot of time mining social media if that's not where your donors, prospects, and advocates are. A university, art museum, or public radio station might find social media a rich pool within which to fish, whereas a locally based literacy program might not.

Content Curation

Most of us are familiar with what the word *curation* means. At some point we've all been to a museum's curated exhibit. Museums hire curators whose job it is to pull together works of art from other areas of the museum, other museums, private collections, and so on to tell a specific story. The curator carefully selects, arranges, and labels all of the works on exhibit so that you can walk through and learn and enjoy that story.

The prospect research field and others have been curating information by hand for a long time. David Lamb was among the first prospect researchers to create webpages that listed the best sites online for finding information about prospects. As soon as the Adobe Acrobat Reader was launched, creating the PDF, a free, common format for reading documents online, websites could curate link lists, white papers, and articles on how to use and conduct research. With the advent of blogs, podcasts, and other tools there are now prospect research websites that have curated a host of useful information on prospect research.

But advances in the latest software technology allow anyone to be a curator of content. From Clipboard to Curata, Scoop.it to Storify, and Paper.li to Pinterest, information curation websites are popping up at a fast pace. As with most new software, right now they are more often free or low-cost to encourage adoption. A curation website is powered by software that allows you choose your online content sources and create a webpage or newspaper type page that can be shared with others.

For example, if you are interested in keeping up with prospect research you could use Paper.li to create an online "newspaper." You might decide to include stories from Twitter that have the hashtag #prospectresearch, articles from the *Chronicle of Philanthropy* and other news sources, and some of your favorite blog posts. The curation website gives you a list of all the articles that meet your criteria and you select exactly which ones to include in your newspaper. Presto! You now have a newspaper you can share on Twitter, e-mail to your colleagues, or even share with stakeholders.

These new curation websites allow you to pull together a powerful suite of information with just a few clicks. You do not have to read a lot of print newspapers and magazines, search the Internet, and stay painstakingly up-to-date with your online reading. Suddenly you can select good content with things like key words and hashtags.

Automated curation has the advantage of being fast and easy, but just as with any curation project, the time and effort spent—or lack thereof—is often obvious in the result. For example, a newspaper created through Paper.li requires you to establish content sources and search criteria, select which results should be included in the newspaper edition, and create your presentation format. To be a sought-after read, this kind of automated content curation requires adherence to fundamental marketing principles: Know your audience, deliver solid content, and be consistent. If your search terms are too broad, your content sources are not credible, or any of your execution is sloppy, your curated content falls on the side of data overload and will likely be ignored.

Prospect research is a specialized field in fundraising that adapts quickly to technology. The creative and productive uses for automated content curation in the future are many and varied. Here are some examples of how prospect research has used content curation in real life.

CASE STUDY

STARTING WITH JUST A HELPFUL WEB PAGE OR TWO

Andrea Graves at the University of California, San Diego created a web page with a calendar of training opportunities, meetings, contact information, and resources for the internal use of the development division. Her colleagues use the site to sign up for trainings, download podcasts, and view recorded seminars. They can submit a research request or find basic information using the links on the page.

Al Gabor at Northwestern University and Gray Cargill at the University of Vermont curate two of a number of well-regarded prospect research resource pages containing hundreds of valuable links used by prospect researchers and other fundraisers worldwide.

At the Helen Brown Group (this book's co-author's company), we create a purpose-built web page for each of the clients that we work with on a dedicated basis. This page contains RSS feeds, news alerts, useful research links, search boxes, blogs of interest, and curated articles on topics relevant to each client. We also include a listing of all completed and outstanding work for the month. Clients can check in on the status of their requests or use the site as a portal for more information about prospects, topics or issues they are interested in.

Tools like these give us an amazing ability to manage the information that surrounds and threatens to drown us sometimes. Keeping up with and using these tools is time-intensive, so it is important to be clear on what you hope to accomplish, but their potential uses can be powerful:

- What about creating a site with curated information to engage with donors and volunteers?
- Would it be helpful to have a resource for internal use so that everyone in your fundraising operation is aware of big news?

CONTENT CURATION IN ACTION

Molly Carocci of Beth Israel Deaconess Medical Center uses Scoop.it to curate a web resource called "Prospect Research in Nonprofit Fundraising." Molly gathers articles from sources like *Forbes*, the *Chronicle of Philanthropy*, *Barron's*, and several philanthropy-related blogs and adds her own commentary to pull out the salient features of each article. Those articles are then available in an easy-to-read page for anyone to reference.

Question: How long have you had your Scoop.it page?

Answer: Since October 2011.

Q: What made you decide to create it?

A: I had read about new tools for content curation, and I had also been thinking about blogging. I use Scoop.it is as a way to combine content curation and content creation (e.g., blogging). Scoop.it is quick, easy, and shiny.

Q: How do you decide which articles to highlight?

A: Scoop.it feeds content to me based on my specified criteria related to prospect research, and I can post content as-is, or add my own commentary. I also choose articles from my personal search alerts. I post items or articles that I think would be of interest to a general prospect research or fundraising audience, although some-times I'll slip in something just because I like it. I follow several other Scoop.it feeds related to fundraising, content curation, and Finland

(Continued)

(just because). Sometimes I'll "re-scoop" a post from someone else's page (similar to "re-tweeting"), but usually I find my own content.

Q: Did you set it up to be a resource to the fundraisers in your shop or people in fundraising/research generally?

A: I started it as an experiment, really, to see if I could commit to an ongoing online project, learn a new tool, and be more social. My intention was to keep it private initially, and then when it was good enough, start sharing it. But Scoop.it had no privacy option! So I got over myself pretty quickly. I then wanted it to be suitable for a wider audience of fundraisers and non-profit workers as well as researchers.

Q: Can people follow it? How?

A: Anyone can follow it by going to www.scoop.it/t/prospect -research-in-non-profit-fundraising. You can receive e-mail alerts when I've posted a new article.

Q: What is the coolest thing about your Scoop.it page (or Scoop.it generally?)

A: Scoop.it makes it possible for anyone to quickly and easily create a professional-looking online "magazine." It's free, with some fee-based analytics. The coolest thing about my page is that it was the first one to cover prospect research, and I hope that it's useful.

Q: Do you see any trends evolving out of this?

A: Content curation is another aspect of social media that is getting more robust as the audience grows and new tools are developed to drive great content. Scoop.it increases content exposure by allowing curators to link posts to their profiles on Facebook, Google+, LinkedIn, Pinterest, StumbleUpon, and Twitter. Other tools do this also: Storify, Bundlr, Paper.li, et cetera.

And many of these tools are going mobile, adding to their potential user bases. The Pew Internet and American Life Project recently gave a presentation, "Mobile is the Needle, Social is the Thread: How Information Today is Woven into Our Lives" (which I found via Scoop.it). According to their data, we're living in a time of converging ubiquity (my term, not theirs), where social networking sites, information, population, and technology are all available and interacting at an increasing rate. The signal-to-noise ratio is more skewed toward noise, so pulling relevant information out of all the junk is more important than it's ever been.

WHAT THE FUTURE MIGHT LOOK LIKE

In this chapter we have covered many related trends. Now let's imagine how we might combine them to make information timely and meaningful to the frontline fundraiser of the future.

Imagine George is preparing for a visit with Mr. and Mrs. Gable he has scheduled for the next day. He opens up the prospect record in the database and reviews the information, including what has been researched. Then he clicks on a link and is taken to a web page that has the following information:

- Headlines about every company and organization with which Mr. and Mrs. Gable are affiliated.
- Gifts they have made to other organizations in the past six months.
- Useful articles, tweets, and blog posts about "Empty Nesters" relating to giving preferences and their lifestyle.
- A few statistics about the universities where their two children are enrolled.
- A picture of their home with a link to directions.

George might have seen their most recent social media posts, too, but this couple happens not to participate at all in social media. Once George is finished viewing this information, he goes back to the database record and clicks another link that takes him to an internal webpage on Mr. and Mrs. Gable. This one shows him the following information:

- A line graph showing the largest donor to the organization, the lowest entry-level major gift, and where Mr. and Mrs. Gable fit in with their past giving and the proposed ask amount.
- Visuals demonstrating Mr. and Mrs. Gable's pattern of giving to the organization by date and amount.
- A bar chart demonstrating which projects Mr. and Mrs. Gable have given to.
- A relationship map of the people to whom they are connected allowing George to click to change the type of relationship and zoom in or out.

George knows Mr. and Mrs. Gable are very close to one of the professors, so he goes back into the database's "relationships" function and opens the professor's record. From there he can click to an internal webpage that shows him the following information on the professor:

- A picture of the professor with a link to a biography and the professor's school and research page.
- Internal and external news about the professor and his research work.
- Any social media feeds including Twitter and blogs.

It is the end of the day and George checks his dashboard one more time. He can see that this meeting with Mr. and Mrs. Gable will meet his minimum face-to-face visits for the month and he still has three more scheduled! He walks out of the office for the evening with a smile on his face. He also has his iPad tucked under his arm, from which he can access all of the same information from anywhere he happens to be.

SUMMARY

Technology changes quickly and frequently. The majority of the tools and applications we take for granted in our everyday life today didn't exist five years ago. That's one of the things that makes prospect research such an exciting and interesting field, and the reason why continuing education to stay abreast of new developments is so important.

Watching other industries and how they use technology has always informed our work as prospect researchers. Market research in the corporate world led to the advent of prospect research as a field and analytics as a discipline. Customer relationship management systems (CRMs) in corporate sales departments led the way for increasingly intelligent and complex databases to track and manage the relationship between our nonprofits and donors.

Big data and segmentation reflect the fact that information in the online world is exploding and the companies and organizations that can take advantage of it will be more successful in relationship building and fundraising. As we begin to live more and more in the world of data, visual solutions are beginning to make it easier to understand the human side of the data story. Data visualization can take many forms, including relationship mapping, which provides an obvious benefit in major gift fundraising. Social scoring and content curation represent other efforts to make sense of the data avalanche. However, no matter what new tools are created to help us accomplish our tasks, the basic fundraising principles have not changed. Prospect research tools are designed and used to engage and deepen the relationship an organization has with its donors, friends and beneficiaries. Every time there is any kind of shift, whether it is in the economy, in the environment, in social attitudes, or somewhere else, nonprofit organizations of every size have to be able to focus more clearly on gaining, keeping, and deepening their donor relationships.

As you have probably noted after reading this book, prospect research hinges on data, and every sized organization can suffer from poorly planned data management or benefit from a strong data system. If you need to identify, track, and research your prospects or if you want to take advantage of some of the trends gaining traction in fundraising, you must ensure your organization does the following:

- Captures and maintains data accurately.
- Knows what fundraising questions need to be answered.
- Possesses the resources to get and present the answers that you need to fundraise well.

If you can manage your data well, you can benefit from prospect research. And the good news is that prospect research is becoming more accessible to the end user. In the future, the end user is likely to be receiving current information on-demand, from anywhere, and on any device that has Internet access.

FOR FURTHER READING

Aaker, Jennifer Lynn, Andy Smith, and Carlye Adler. *The Dragonfly Effect: Quick, Effective, and Powerful Ways to Use Social Media to Drive Social Change*. San Francisco: Jossey-Bass, 2010.

Kanter, Beth, and Allison H. Fine. *The Networked Nonprofit: Connecting with Social Media to Drive Change*. San Francisco: Jossey-Bass, 2010.

Kanter, Beth, and Katie Delahaye Paine. *Measuring the Networked Nonprofit: Using Data to Change the World*. San Francisco: Jossey-Bass, 2012.

Rosenbaum, Steven C. *Curation Nation: How to Win in a World Where Consumers Are Creators*. New York: McGraw-Hill, 2011.

Schaefer, Mark. *Return on Influence: The Revolutionary Power of Klout, Social Scoring, and Influence Marketing*. New York: McGraw-Hill, 2012.

AFP Code of Ethical Principles and Standards

ETHICAL PRINCIPLES • Adopted 1964; amended Sept. 2007

The Association of Fundraising Professionals (AFP) exists to foster the development and growth of fundraising professionals and the profession, to promote high ethical behavior in the fundraising profession and to preserve and enhance philanthropy and volunteerism. Members of AFP are motivated by an inner drive to improve the quality of life through the causes they serve. They serve the ideal of philanthropy, are committed to the preservation and enhancement of volunteerism; and hold stewardship of these concepts as the overriding direction of their professional life. They recognize their responsibility to ensure that needed resources are vigorously and ethically sought and that the intent of the donor is honestly fulfilled. To these ends, AFP members, both individual and business, embrace certain values that they strive to uphold in performing their responsibilities for generating philanthropic support. AFP business members strive to promote and protect the work and mission of their client organizations.

AFP members both individual and business aspire to:

- practice their profession with integrity, honesty, truthfulness and adherence to the absolute obligation to safeguard the public trust
- act according to the highest goals and visions of their organizations, professions, clients and consciences
- put philanthropic mission above personal gain;
- inspire others through their own sense of dedication and high purpose
- improve their professional knowledge and skills, so that their performance will better serve others
- demonstrate concern for the interests and well-being of individuals affected by their actions
- value the privacy, freedom of choice and interests of all those affected by their actions
- foster cultural diversity and pluralistic values and treat all people with dignity and respect
- affirm, through personal giving, a commitment to p   hilanthropy and its role in society
- adhere to the spirit as well as the letter of all applicable laws and regulations
- advocate within their organizations adherence to all applicable laws and regulations
- avoid even the appearance of any criminal offense or professional misconduct
- bring credit to the fundraising profession by their public demeanor
- encourage colleagues to embrace and practice these ethical principles and standards
- be aware of the codes of ethics promulgated by other professional organizations that serve philanthropy

ETHICAL STANDARDS

Furthermore, while striving to act according to the above values, AFP members, both individual and business, agree to abide (and to ensure, to the best of their ability, that all members of their staff abide) by the AFP standards. Violation of the standards may subject the member to disciplinary sanctions, including expulsion, as provided in the AFP Ethics Enforcement Procedures.

MEMBER OBLIGATIONS

1. Members shall not engage in activities that harm the members' organizations, clients or profession.
2. Members shall not engage in activities that conflict with their fiduciary, ethical and legal obligations to their organizations, clients or profession.
3. Members shall effectively disclose all potential and actual conflicts of interest; such disclosure does not preclude or imply ethical impropriety.
4. Members shall not exploit any relationship with a donor, prospect, volunteer, client or employee for the benefit of the members or the members' organizations.
5. Members shall comply with all applicable local, state, provincial and federal civil and criminal laws.
6. Members recognize their individual boundaries of competence and are forthcoming and truthful about their professional experience and qualifications and will represent their achievements accurately and without exaggeration.
7. Members shall present and supply products and/or services honestly and without misrepresentation and will clearly identify the details of those products, such as availability of the products and/or services and other factors that may affect the suitability of the products and/or services for donors, clients or nonprofit organizations.
8. Members shall establish the nature and purpose of any contractual relationship at the outset and will be responsive and available to organizations and their employing organizations before, during and after any sale of materials and/or services. Members will comply with all fair and reasonable obligations created by the contract.

9. Members shall refrain from knowingly infringing the intellectual property rights of other parties at all times. Members shall address and rectify any inadvertent infringement that may occur.
10. Members shall protect the confidentiality of all privileged information relating to the provider/client relationships.
11. Members shall refrain from any activity designed to disparage competitors untruthfully.

SOLICITATION AND USE OF PHILANTHROPIC FUNDS

12. Members shall take care to ensure that all solicitation and communication materials are accurate and correctly reflect their organizations' mission and use of solicited funds.
13. Members shall take care to ensure that donors receive informed, accurate and ethical advice about the value and tax implications of contributions.
14. Members shall take care to ensure that contributions are used in accordance with donors' intentions.
15. Members shall take care to ensure proper stewardship of all revenue sources, including timely reports on the use and management of such funds.
16. Members shall obtain explicit consent by donors before altering the conditions of financial transactions.

PRESENTATION OF INFORMATION

17. Members shall not disclose privileged or confidential information to unauthorized parties.
18. Members shall adhere to the principle that all donor and prospect information created by, or on behalf of, an organization or a client is the property of that organization or client and shall not be transferred or utilized except on behalf of that organization or client.
19. Members shall give donors and clients the opportunity to have their names removed from lists that are sold to, rented to or exchanged with other organizations.
20. Members shall, when stating fundraising results, use accurate and consistent accounting methods that conform to the appropriate guidelines adopted by the American Institute of Certified Public Accountants (AICPA)* for the type of organization involved. (* In countries outside of the United States, comparable authority should be utilized.)

COMPENSATION AND CONTRACTS

21. Members shall not accept compensation or enter into a contract that is based on a percentage of contributions; nor shall members accept finder's fees or contingent fees. Business members must refrain from receiving compensation from third parties derived from products or services for a client without disclosing that third-party compensation to the client (for example, volume rebates from vendors to business members).
22. Members may accept performance-based compensation, such as bonuses, provided such bonuses are in accord with prevailing practices within the members' own organizations and are not based on a percentage of contributions.
23. Members shall neither offer nor accept payments or special considerations for the purpose of influencing the selection of products or services.
24. Members shall not pay finder's fees, commissions or percentage compensation based on contributions, and shall take care to discourage their organizations from making such payments.
25. Any member receiving funds on behalf of a donor or client must meet the legal requirements for the disbursement of those funds. Any interest or income earned on the funds should be fully disclosed.

A Donor Bill of Rights

PHILANTHROPY is based on voluntary action for the common good. It is a tradition of giving and sharing that is primary to the quality of life. To assure that philanthropy merits the respect and trust of the general public, and that donors and prospective donors can have full confidence in the not-for-profit organizations and causes they are asked to support, we declare that all donors have these rights:

I.

To be informed of the organization's mission, of the way the organization intends to use donated resources, and of its capacity to use donations effectively for their intended purposes.

II.

To be informed of the identity of those serving on the organization's governing board, and to expect the board to exercise prudent judgement in its stewardship responsibilities.

III.

To have access to the organization's most recent financial statements.

IV.

To be assured their gifts will be used for the purposes for which they were given.

V.

To receive appropriate acknowledgement and recognition.

VI.

To be assured that information about their donations is handled with respect and with confidentiality to the extent provided by law.

VII.

To expect that all relationships with individuals representing organizations of interest to the donor will be professional in nature.

VIII.

To be informed whether those seeking donations are volunteers, employees of the organization or hired solicitors.

IX.

To have the opportunity for their names to be deleted from mailing lists that an organization may intend to share.

X.

To feel free to ask questions when making a donation and to receive prompt, truthful and forthright answers.

DEVELOPED BY	ENDORSED BY
	(in formation)
	Independent Sector
Association of Fundraising Professionals (AFP)	National Catholic Development Conference (NCDC)
Association for Healthcare Philanthropy (AHP)	National Committee on Planned Giving (NCPG)
Council for Advancement and Support of Education (CASE)	Council for Resource Development (CRD)
Giving Institute: Leading Consultants to Non-Profits	United Way of America

Appendix C: APRA Statement of Ethics[1]

Association of Professional Researchers for Advancement (APRA)

Statement of Ethics In 2008 the APRA board charged the Ethics Committee to prepare an updated revision of APRA's Statement of Ethics, focusing on the broad essentials of ethics rather than the details of our day-to-day work. In response, the committee reviewed the code of ethics of many fundraising associations and research organizations and drafted a new statement that focused on what committee members considered to the four essentials of ethical conduct: personal integrity, accountability, practice, and conflict of interest. The board approved the statement in December 2008.

APRA members shall support and further the individual's fundamental right to privacy and protect the confidential information of their institutions. APRA members are committed to the ethical collection and use of information. Members shall follow all applicable national, state, and local laws, as well as institutional policies, governing the collection, use, maintenance, and dissemination of information in the pursuit of the missions of their institutions.

Code of Ethics Advancement researchers must balance an individual's right to privacy with the needs of their institutions to collect, analyze, record, maintain, use, and disseminate information. This balance is not always easy to maintain. To guide researchers, the following ethical principles apply:

Preamble Establishing and maintaining ethical and professional standards is a primary goal of the mission of the Association of Professional

---

[1]Copyright 2009 by the Association of Professional Researchers for Advancement. Revised December 2009.

Researchers for Advancement (APRA). All APRA members shall support and further an individual's fundamental right to privacy and protect the confidential information of their institutions. All members agree to abide by this Statement of Ethics in the daily conduct of all professional activity encompassing the gathering, dissemination, and use of information for the purposes of fundraising or other institutional advancement activity.

Four fundamental principles provide the foundation for the ethical conduct of fundraising research, relationship management, and analytics: integrity, accountability, practice, and conflict of interest.

Integrity   Members shall be truthful with respect to their identities and purpose and the identity of their institutions during the course of their work. They shall continually strive to increase the recognition and respect of the profession.

Accountability   Members shall respect the privacy of donors and prospects and conduct their work with the highest level of discretion. They shall adhere to the spirit as well as the letter of all applicable laws and all policies of their organization. They shall conduct themselves in the utmost professional manner in accordance with the standards of their organization.

Practice   Members shall take the necessary care to ensure that their work is as accurate as possible. They shall only record data that is appropriate to the fundraising process and protect the confidentiality of all personal information at all times.

Conflicts of Interest   Members shall avoid competing professional or personal interests and shall disclose such interests to their institutions at the first instance. A conflict of interest can create an appearance of impropriety that can undermine confidence in the member, their organization, and the profession.

Appendix D: APRA Skill Sets—Advanced

Partners in Fundraising

The APRA Skills Set: Advanced Prospect Research
Updated January 26, 2005

Introduction

The APRA Skills Sets are designed to help advancement professionals and human resource professionals design job descriptions, training programs, and performance evaluation tools for prospect research professionals. Since development organizations come in many forms, it is important to note that the APRA Skills Sets are recommendations that should be customized to meet the specific needs of each institution.

At present, the APRA Skills Sets are comprised of four individual Skills Sets. The first, Prospect Research Fundamentals, focuses on the skills that should be acquired by an advancement prospect researcher in the early part of his or her training. The second, Advanced Prospect Research, builds on Prospect Research Fundamentals and outlines skills required for advanced prospect research work. The third, Research Management, is a distinct set that does not build on the first two, but instead outlines the skills required for the management of a prospect research operation. The fourth, Relationship Management, is a second distinct set that does not build on the first two. This skills set outlines the skills required for a professional whose job is comprised solely of relationship management responsibilities.

Definition of Terms

The APRA Skills Sets use the following terms to describe the proficiency levels. The proficiencies build upon each other and assume that preceding proficiencies have been attained.

Information Proficiencies

- *Awareness:* Individual can recognize terms and has broad understanding of meanings; actual practice may be minimal and infrequent; could not instruct others.
- *Understanding:* Individual comprehends the philosophy supporting the issue, policy, or procedure
- *Knowledge:* Individual has a significant grasp of details, specifics, and shades of meaning, could present information to colleagues inside and outside of development

Skill Proficiencies

- *Ability:* Individual is trained, but not experienced at accomplishing the activity
- *Proficiency:* Individual has developed skill using industry and institutional best practices; practice has been intense and/or frequent
- *Mastery:* Individual has comprehensive grasp of task details, specific procedures, and task's connection to strategic objectives; practice has been intense and/or frequent; could instruct colleagues

The Advanced Research Skills Set assumes that all proficiencies in the Prospect Research Fundamentals have been achieved. **The Advanced Research Skills Set is comprised, therefore, of all components of the Prospect Research Fundamentals Skills Set and five additional categories.**

1. Advanced General Fundraising
2. Advanced Prospect Research
3. Relationship Management
4. Resources
5. Advanced Professional Skills

Note: For the purposes of this document, the terms "relationship management" and "prospect management" are interchangeable.

Advanced General Fundraising

- Understanding of outright and deferred giving vocabulary, vehicles, and strategy
- Understanding of ever-changing trends in fundraising and philanthropy, within your organization as well as in the broader context
- Understanding of how the governing board functions within your organization and what role the board serves in fundraising
- Knowledge of organization's history and mission; strong ability to articulate same
- Knowledge of a broad array of fundraising practices and procedures
- Ability to apply appropriate fundraising strategies to projects
- Ability to analyze and match charitable and economic interests of prospective donors and to properly profile donor prospects from a fundraising perspective

Advanced Prospect Research

- Knowledge of and ability to utilize IRS statistical net wealth estimation data
- Knowledge of the establishment and use of private personal and family foundations, including the ability to identify and interpret the key informational areas of an IRS Form 990 and Form 990-PF, including (but not limited to) header; reporting date; total asset base as of reporting date; asset description and valuation; gift history and giving patterns over time
- Knowledge of multiple screening strategies and methodologies, including (but not limited to) constituent list segmentation on the basis of limited, specific variables such as zip code, giving history, age, sex, or other demographic data; external, electronic database screening; and peer group screening
- Ability to find and use a wide variety of digital and print resources
- Ability to read and interpret legal documents commonly used at the organization's prospect research operation as appropriate
- Ability to find and evaluate evidence of philanthropic interests in other organizations
- Ability to identify and present information about luxury items and collections, including estimated value, importance to the prospect, and relevance to one's organization
- Ability to employ a wide variety of proactive prospecting methodologies, including but not limited to the following:
  o Ability to perform in-house data mining, including sophisticated constituent database queries and a strong understanding of statistical modeling concepts
  o Ability to use mailing and contact lists from other sources, such as list houses, other organizations, and internet searches, particularly to identify interest categories and affiliations appropriate to specific organizational goals or projects
- Mastery of all aspects of real property research, including issues such as assessment vs. market value and property history as well as financing strategies and general market conditions
- Mastery of SEC data, including elements such as compensation information contained in proxies and 10K reports; insider stock options, ownership, and transfers; business interlocks; specific reporting relationships; and accurate evaluation of profit and loss and business forecast statements
- Mastery in accurately analyzing, interpreting, and evaluating information collected about a donor prospect, coupled with great skill in both written and verbal communication of both the essential data and the final interpretation of its meaning
- Mastery of general fundraising strategies, which may be appropriate to the donor prospect in the identification-cultivation-solicitation-stewardship cycle of fundraising and the ability to offer strategic suggestions and approaches

Relationship Management

- Ability to orient and train colleagues on the principals of relationship management and the details of the relationship management system
- Ability to serve as a liaison between development staff and technical staff for the development and execution of queries, reports, and other relationship management tools
- Ability to facilitate and coordinate definition of relationship management policies and procedures
- Proficiency with constituent segmentation strategies
- Proficiency with retrieving and analyzing prospect data to inform cultivation strategies as well as individual and team-level prospect pool management
- Mastery of organization's prospect tracking and management systems, including relationship management data entry, queries, and reports

Resources

- Understanding of current privacy laws, such as HIPAA
- Understanding of information management issues, trends, and tools
- Knowledge of changing market of subscription-based research resources such as electronic wealth-screening services, news databases, and business directories
- Ability to assess quality of resources and make recommendations that are most appropriate for specific information needs
- Ability to maintain information management systems, hard-copy and electronic. Highly developed ability to identify, evaluate, and utilize new or alternative resources for information, including text sources, electronic sources, and screening results. In particular, thorough review of source validity and the creative use of sources as applied to the process of evaluating donor prospects for capacity, inclination, and readiness
- Mastery of in-house resources and all proprietary information systems
- Mastery of privacy policies of professional organizations such as APRA, AFP, AHP, and CASE, and expertise of organization's internal privacy policies

Advanced Professional Skills

- Knowledge of organization's job and performance evaluation process
- Knowledge of principles of management, leadership, conflict resolution, negotiation and motivation
- Knowledge of solicitation strategy and major gifts process
- Ability to work with development officers to help build prospect strategy
- Ability to teach basic prospect research skills to a diverse audience (this includes making public oral presentations, designing and implementing formal training on basic prospect research, and mentoring up-and-coming researchers)
- Ability to liaise with development officers in order to anticipate and respond to needs of information and information management needs
- Ability to demonstrate commitment to adhere to all legal privacy requirements and all ethical standards upheld by organizations such as APRA, AFP, AHP, and CASE
- Ability to demonstrate commitment to promoting or advocating prospect research (this involves proactively seeking opportunities for researchers to be involved in development activities within an organization, and promoting prospect research within the fundraising profession)
- Ability to demonstrate commitment to professional development, including attending regional professional events, participating in a mentor/mentee relationship, or seeking other professional education opportunities

© 2005 APRA

APPENDIX E: APRA SKILL SETS—FUNDAMENTALS

Partners in Fundraising

The APRA Skills Set: Prospect Research Fundamentals
Updated January 26, 2005

Introduction

The APRA Skills Sets are designed to help advancement professionals and human resource professionals design job descriptions, training programs, and performance evaluation tools for prospect research professionals. Since development organizations come in many forms, it is important to note that the APRA Skills Sets are recommendations that should be customized to meet the specific needs of each institution.

At present, the APRA Skills Sets are comprised of four individual Skills Sets. The first, Prospect Research Fundamentals, focuses on the skills that should be acquired by an advancement prospect researcher in the early part of his or her training. The second, Advanced Prospect Research, builds on Prospect Research Fundamentals and outlines skills required for advanced prospect research work. The third, Research Management, is a distinct set that does not build on the first two, but instead outlines the skills required for the management of a prospect research operation. The fourth, Relationship Management, is a second distinct set that does not build on the first two. This skills set outlines the skills required for a professional whose job is comprised solely of relationship management responsibilities.

Definition of Terms

The APRA Skills Sets use the following terms to describe the proficiency levels. The proficiencies build upon each other and assume that preceding proficiencies have been attained.

Information Proficiencies

- _Awareness:_ Individual can recognize terms and has broad understanding of meanings; actual practice may be minimal and infrequent; could not instruct others
- _Understanding:_ Individual comprehends the philosophy supporting the issue, policy, or procedure
- _Knowledge:_ Individual has a significant grasp of details, specifics, and shades of meaning, could present information to colleagues inside and outside of development

Skill Proficiencies

- _Ability:_ Individual is trained, but not experienced at accomplishing the activity
- _Proficiency:_ Individual has developed skill using industry and institutional best practices; practice has been intense and/or frequent
- _Mastery:_ Individual has comprehensive grasp of task details, specific procedures, and task's connection to strategic objectives; practice has been intense and/or frequent; could instruct colleagues

The Prospect Research Fundamentals Skills Set is comprised of five categories:

1. Institutional Knowledge
2. General Fundraising Knowledge
3. General Research and Resource Fundamentals
4. Prospect Research Fundamentals
5. Professional Fundamentals

Institutional Knowledge

- Understanding of your organization's mission, history, programs, and operational strategy
- Understanding of your organization's fundraising needs, goals, and development philosophy
- Understanding of your organization's culture, organizational structure, and administrative processes and procedures
- Knowledge of your organization's case for support

General Fundraising Knowledge

- Understanding of central issues in the field of philanthropy and the motivations behind charitable giving
- Understanding of the difference between gifts to endowments, capital purposes, and operating budgets (annual funds)
- Understanding of the different units within overall fundraising programs. These programs may include annual giving/membership, campaigns (capital, endowment, and comprehensive), major gift fundraising, planned gift fundraising, grant writing, gift records, and stewardship
- Understanding of various jobs and responsibilities among staff in all fundraising programs.
- Knowledge of how different fundraising programs require different support and services from prospect researchers
- Knowledge of donor types: Individual, estate, corporate, foundation, and government
- Knowledge of cultivation process/cycle: identification, qualification, cultivation, sight-setting, solicitation, and stewardship
- Knowledge with relevant ethics policies (such as CASE, AFP or AHP) and the Donor Bill of Rights
- Mastery of and compliance with the APRA Ethics Statement

General Research & Resource Fundamentals

- Understanding of what constitutes relevant and strategic information and how to analyze that information to support prospect development
- Understanding of information management in a database structure, particularly the ability to store, manipulate, and retrieve data
- Understanding of the difference between proactive research (taking the initiative in identifying and qualifying prospects) and reactive research (responding to directives or requests for research)
- Knowledge of parameters (legal and institutional) regarding what information is public and ethical to use
- Knowledge of primary resource providers (electronic vs. text, government and commercial, internal and external) and the type and scope available from each
- Proficiency in identifying and utilizing additional resources such as librarians, government employees, colleagues, and constituents (including donors and volunteers) when appropriate
- Proficiency in utilizing all resources available, including an awareness of different search techniques and mastery of Boolean searching
- Proficiency in determining the quality, reliability, and accuracy of sources
- Proficiency in acquiring cost-effective, appropriate, and sound information

Prospect Research Fundamentals

- Understanding the roles that prospect information and prospect research play in prospect development throughout the prospect cultivation cycle:
  - o Identification – locating Information
  - o Qualification – analyzing information
  - o Cultivation – interpreting information
  - o Solicitation – applying information
  - o Stewardship – applying information
- Proficiency in evaluating prospects by financial capacity, interests, and relationships
- Proficiency in recognizing wealth indicators (such as real estate, public company stock holdings, salary data, private company value, foundation assets, collections, hobbies, other philanthropic activity, etc.) and liabilities (such as tuitions, lifestyles, personal issues, etc.)
- Proficiency in evaluating financial assets and known liabilities to estimate prospect giving potential and apply appropriate ratings, specifically:
  - o Real Estate: Understanding the difference between market value and assessed value of real estate in name or in trust; ability to calculate and/or estimate market value for a property.
  - o Public Companies: Ability to calculate insider stock holdings and options values
  - o Private Companies: Ability to calculate or estimate the value of a prospect's ownership in a private company using comparison and industry data
  - o Foundations: Understanding the different types of foundations (independent, private, family, operating, corporate, community); Knowledge of the IRS forms 990-PF and 990 and the information found within these documents

Professional Fundamentals

- Knowledge of available training and educational opportunities to develop skills and to keep abreast of trends within the profession
- Proficiency in writing clearly and concisely
- Proficiency in synthesizing material from multiple sources into a coherent and accurate presentation
- Proficiency in communicating effectively with diverse audiences in conversations and through documents
- Proficiency in responding to requests and obtaining information in a timely manner.
- Proficiency in conducting an informational interview with people who request information and with those from whom information is sought
- Proficiency in listening skills
- Proficiency in independent work
- Proficiency in working jointly with colleagues in a team effort to reach organizational goals

© 2005 APRA

APPENDIX F: APRA SKILL SETS—RELATIONSHIP MANAGEMENT

Partners in Fundraising

The APRA Skills Set: Relationship Management
August 2005

Introduction

The APRA Skills Sets are designed to help advancement professionals and human resource professionals design job descriptions, training programs, and performance evaluation tools for advancement prospect research professionals. Since development organizations come in many forms, it is important to note that the APRA Skills Sets are recommendations that should be customized to meet the specific needs of each institution.

At present, the APRA Skills Sets are comprised of four individual Skills Sets. The first, Prospect Research Fundamentals, focuses on the skills that should be acquired by an advancement prospect researcher in the early part of his or her training. The second, Advanced Prospect Research, builds on Prospect Research Fundamentals and outlines skills required for advanced prospect research work. The third, Research Management, is a distinct set that does not build on the first two, but instead outlines the skills required for the management of a prospect research operation. The fourth, Relationship Management, is a second distinct set that does not build on the first two. This skills set outlines the skills required for a professional whose job is comprised solely of relationship management responsibilities.

NOTE: For the purposes of this document, the terms "relationship management" and "prospect management" are interchangeable.

Definition of Terms

The APRA Skills Sets use the following terms to describe the proficiency levels. The proficiencies build upon each other, and assume that preceding proficiencies have been attained.

Information Proficiencies

- *Awareness:* Individual can recognize terms and has broad understanding of meanings; actual practice may be minimal and infrequent; could not instruct others.
- *Understanding:* Individual comprehends the philosophy supporting the issue, policy, or procedure
- *Knowledge:* Individual has a significant grasp of details, specifics, and shades of meaning; could present information to colleagues inside and outside of development

Skill Proficiencies

- *Ability:* Individual is trained but not experienced at accomplishing the activity
- *Proficiency:* Individual has developed skill using industry and institutional best practices; practice has been intense and/or frequent
- *Mastery:* Individual has comprehensive grasp of task details, specific procedures, and task's connection to strategic objectives; practice has been intense and/or frequent; could instruct colleagues

The Relationship Management Skills Set is a distinct Skills Set, and does not assume that all proficiencies in the Prospect Research Fundamentals and Advanced Research Skills Sets have been achieved. The Relationship Management Skills Set is comprised of six categories:

1. Prospect Research Fundamentals
2. Relationship Management
3. Systems
4. Institutional Knowledge
5. General Fundraising
6. Professional Development

Recommendations: Relationship management professionals need to know prospect research fundamentals.

Note: Any individual may have jobs that share the responsibility of prospect research and relationship management.

Prospect Research Fundamentals

- Knowledge of the roles that prospect information and prospect research play in prospect development throughout the prospect cultivation cycle
  o Identification – locating Information
  o Qualification – analyzing information
  o Cultivation – interpreting information
  o Solicitation – applying information
  o Stewardship – applying information

- Understanding of standard prospect research procedures and products

  NOTE: For relationship managers who do this full time, this is sufficient. For those who do a combination, that is, for those who also have responsibilities in prospect research, please refer to the Prospect Research Skills Set and the Advanced Prospect Research Skills Set

Relationship Management

- Knowledge of the institution's constituent and prospect pools (demographics, ratings, philanthropic interests, etc.) as a whole
- Proficiency in delivering information clearly to others on the institutions constituent and prospect pools in written (table and chart) and oral (presentations) form
- Proficiency in utilizing prospect research data to make recommendations for prospect activity
- Proficiency in designing and analyzing gift pyramids and campaign fundraising reports
- Proficiency in orientating and training colleagues on the principals of relationship management and the details of the relationship management system
- Proficiency in interpersonal skills required to serve as a liaison between development staff and technical staff for the development and execution of queries, reports, and other relationship management tools
- Proficiency with facilitation and coordination skills required to define clear relationship management policies and procedures
- Mastery of constituent segmentation strategies
- Mastery of prospect data retrieval and analysis to inform cultivation strategies as well as individual and team-level prospect pool management
- Mastery of organization's prospect tracking and management systems, including relationship management data entry, queries, and reports

Systems

- Knowledge of types of data necessary to support the development staff in their overall and day-to-day operations
- Knowledge of the organization's record keeping systems and information retrieval capabilities and protocols
- Proficiency in developing and maintaining a prospect tracking system, including prospect ratings, staff assignments, solicitation goals, and moves
- Proficiency in working with information technology staff to realize information management and reporting objectives
- Proficient in report building, conversion and training; liaisoning between development and information technology staff to interpret Information needs and abilities
- Proficiency with appropriate and institutional relational databases and spreadsheet software
- Mastery of word processing, spreadsheet, and database software for delivery and presentation of information
- Mastery of prospect rating systems options, including how to build a new system which accurately records prospect capacity and inclination, how to utilize existing system to effectively prioritize prospect pool, and how to incorporate external ratings appropriately into internal rating system
- Mastery of shaping a moves management system to institutional needs

Institutional Knowledge

- Awareness of the history of development within the organization's field (arts, education, health, social services, etc.)
- Knowledge of current events within the organization's field and their affect on philanthropy for that field, such as privacy laws for healthcare providers
- Knowledge of role, effect, and integration of prospect information within the organizational operations
- Knowledge of the institution's decision-makers, as well as those individuals and departments that have influence
- Knowledge of benefactors, board leaders, key donors, and volunteers

General Fundraising

- Knowledge of the role the research office plays in the entire fundraising process, from identification through stewardship
- Proficiency in the establishment and administration of relationship management: Experience shaping and implementing the policies for tracking, coding, and reporting on data sets that measurably enhance the performance of fundraising efforts
- Knowledge of gift vehicles: Cash, securities, real estate, in-kind, personal property, and planned gift vehicles such as trusts, bequests, annuities, and pooled income funds
- Knowledge of appropriate fundraising strategies and trends for different constituencies
- Knowledge of volunteer roles, identification, training, recognition, and support
- Understanding of gift counting and reporting standards, definitions, and types
- Understanding of advancement information systems including software and business best practice resources including online, hardcopy, and third-party services
- Mastery of the moves management process with the ability to enforce

Professional Development

- Proficiency in staying abreast of trends in the relationship management and fundraising fields through membership and participation in appropriate professional organizations

Appendix G: APRA Skill Sets—Research Management

Partners in Fundraising

The APRA Skills Set: Research Management
January 26, 2005

Introduction

The APRA Skills Sets are designed to help advancement professionals and human resource professionals design job descriptions, training programs, and performance evaluation tools for prospect research professionals. Since development organizations come in many forms, it is important to note that the APRA Skills Sets are recommendations that should be customized to meet the specific needs of each institution.

At present, the APRA Skills Sets are comprised of four individual Skills Sets. The first, Prospect Research Fundamentals, focuses on the skills that should be acquired by an advancement prospect researcher in the early part of his or her training. The second, Advanced Prospect Research, builds on Prospect Research Fundamentals and outlines skills required for advanced prospect research work. The third, Research Management, is a distinct set that does not build on the first two, but instead outlines the skills required for the management of a prospect research operation. The fourth, Relationship Management, is a second distinct set that does not build on the first two. This skills set outlines the skills required for a professional whose job is comprised solely of relationship management responsibilities.

Definition of Terms

The APRA Skills Sets use the following terms to describe the proficiency levels. The proficiencies build upon each other, and assume that preceding proficiencies have been attained.

Information Proficiencies

- *Awareness:* Individual can recognize terms and has broad understanding of meanings; actual practice may be minimal and infrequent; could not instruct others.
- *Understanding:* Individual comprehends the philosophy supporting the issue, policy, or procedure
- *Knowledge:* Individual has a significant grasp of details, specifics, and shades of meaning, could present information to colleagues inside and outside of development

Skill Proficiencies

- *Ability:* Individual is trained, but not experienced at accomplishing the activity
- *Proficiency:* Individual has developed skill using industry and institutional best practices; practice has been intense and/or frequent
- *Mastery:* Individual has comprehensive grasp of task details, specific procedures, and task's connection to strategic objectives; practice has been intense and/or frequent; could instruct colleagues

The Research Management Skills Set is a distinct Skills Set, and does not assume that all proficiencies in the Prospect Research Fundamentals and Advanced Research Skills Sets have been achieved. **The Research Management Skills Set is comprised of eight categories:**

1. Vision and Leadership
2. Marketing/Advocacy
3. Planning
4. Personnel
5. Systems
6. Institutional Knowledge
7. Professional Development
8. General Prospect Research

NOTE: For the purposes of this document, the terms "relationship management" and "prospect management" are interchangeable.

Vision and Leadership

- Ability to envision potential and to foster enthusiasm and commitment in staff members, in departmental performance, and in institutional accomplishment
- Ability to extrapolate strategic goals from the organization's vision statement
- Ability to lead challenging staff and colleagues
- Ability to set a standard for ethical performance and to provide leadership in establishing organizational policy
- Proficiency at taking responsibility for one's actions and the actions of those managed and supervised
- Proficiency at generating staff ownership and fostering an environment in which employees can act with initiative and take responsibility for creating change
- Proficiency in working with and inspiring trust among one's direct reports, peers, supervisor, and organizational leadership

Marketing/Advocacy

- Proficiency in oral and written communication that:
  - Demonstrates Research Office performance and needs within its unit
  - Promotes the performance, contributions, and needs of the Research Office to the organization by tying them to the organizational mission through data-driven information (reports, written summaries) and by way of interactions with colleagues, senior level fundraising staff, administration, trustees, and constituents
  - Promotes the contributions and industry trends of the research profession to other professionals within their organization as well as to others through participation in professional organizations, contributions to industry publications, and presentations at local, regional, and national conferences
- Knowledge of promoting and implementing training programs (documented and presented) on research practices, data system policies related to prospect information, and development system procedures for appropriate staff, administration, and volunteers

Planning

- Understanding of performance rules-of-thumb, industry standards, and best practices in the creation and implementation of goals and new initiatives
- Knowledge of tools and approaches for internal and external benchmarking
- Proficiency in the ability to establish and implement appropriate organizational and research performance goals, measurements, and evaluations related to Research's participation at each stage of the fundraising process
- Proficiency with the strategic planning process:
  - To connect the day-to-day activities of the Research Office to the support of the organization's larger mission
  - To establish and report on monthly, quarterly, yearly, and campaign goals for prospect identification, research, and management
- Proficiency in devising systems, procedures, and policies that track and report on attainment of organizational and research goals and their relationship to the organizational mission
- Proficiency in anticipating and incorporating development trends into research operations

Budget Management

- Knowledge of budgeting terminology and the organization's annual budget cycle and internal rules for governing the expenditure of the budget
- Proficiency at estimating resource requirements annually for personnel, operations, and capital needs, and operating effectively within the resulting budget
- Ability to research and estimate special project budgets such as for a campaign, an information technology project, or a database screening effort

Personnel

- Ability to create job descriptions that accurately reflect each position's role, responsibilities, and requirements for success
- Proficiency in implementing personnel policies and procedures, including appropriate handling of search processes, completion of performance evaluations, and handling of general personnel issues
- Proficiency at hiring capable individuals well-suited to the position and the organization
- Proficiency in planning for and providing cross-training opportunities and process documentation which allows staff to expand abilities and provide unit continuity
- Proficiency in establishing quality control protocols and balance of work-load responsibilities within the unit

Systems

- Proficiency in developing and maintaining a prospect tracking system
- Knowledge of types of data necessary to support the development staff in their overall and day-to-day operations
- Knowledge of the organization's record-keeping systems and information retrieval capabilities and protocols
- Knowledge of relational databases and spreadsheet software
- Ability to work with information technology staff to realize information management and reporting objectives

Institutional Knowledge

- Awareness of the history of development within the organization's field (arts, education, health, social services, etc.)
- Knowledge of current events within the organization's field and their effect on philanthropy for that field, such as privacy laws for healthcare providers
- Knowledge of role, effect, and integration of prospect information within the organizational operations
- Knowledge of the institution's decision-makers, as well as those individuals and departments that have influence

Professional Development

- Proficiency in staying abreast of trends in the research and fundraising fields through membership and participation in appropriate professional organizations
- Proficiency at developing action plans to achieve measurable improvements in one's leadership performance
- Proficiency at demonstrating and advocating the value of training and professional development in increasing staff productivity, accuracy or other improvements

General Fundraising

- Knowledge of the role the research office plays in the entire fundraising process, from identification through stewardship
- Proficiency in the establishment and administration of relationship management: experience shaping and implementing the policies for tracking, coding, and reporting on data sets that measurably enhance the performance of fundraising efforts
- Proficiency in creating and analyzing gift pyramids and campaign fundraising reports
- Knowledge of gift vehicles: Cash, securities, real estate, in-kind, personal property, and planned gift vehicles such as trusts, bequests, annuities, and pooled-income funds
- Knowledge of appropriate fundraising strategies and trends for different organization types
- Knowledge of volunteer roles, identification, training, recognition, and support
- Understanding of gift counting and reporting standards, definitions and types
- Understanding of advancement information systems including software and business best practices

General Prospect Research

- Proficiency in conceptualizing and implementing prospect identification, research/profiling, and relationship management methodologies to support organizational goals
- Proficiency with the evaluation of gift capacity through standard wealth-assessment formulas derived from such items as income, real estate, insider stockholder data, luxury items, collectible assets, philanthropic activity, and private foundations
- Proficiency with systems of ranking and prioritizing prospects based on giving capacity, interest, and readiness
- Proficiency in turning wealth assessment information into intelligence with direct usefulness for front-line fundraisers, prospect strategies, or solicitation plans
- Knowledge of proactive prospect identification techniques such as data segmentation, third-party database screenings, peer constituency screenings and ratings, and mail and electronic surveying
- Knowledge of prospect research resources including online, hardcopy, and third-party services

© 2005 APRA

About the Authors

JENNIFER J. FILLA

Jennifer Filla operates Aspire Research Group out of Florida, providing prospect research services to organizations across the country. Prior to founding Aspire Research Group she served as Associate Director of Development at the Jefferson Kimmel Cancer Center in Philadelphia, Pennsylvania. She is currently a trustee of the Association of Fundraising Professionals, Suncoast Chapter, and was most recently the 2010–2011 president of the Association of Professional Researchers for Advancement, Florida chapter.

HELEN E. BROWN

Helen Brown is president of The Helen Brown Group LLC and a 20+-year veteran in the field of prospect research. She is a former director of the Association of Professional Researchers for Advancement (APRA) and currently serves as chair of the APRA Chapter Relations Committee. She is a past president of the New England Development Research Association. In 2006 she received the NEDRA Ann Castle Award for service to the prospect research community. Helen also owns ShareTraining, a web-based training company for fundraising professionals. She is a nonexecutive director of the U.K.-based prospect research company Factary Ltd. and is Special Advisor on Fundraising to the North American Foundation for the University of Manchester.

Index

Printed and bound by CPI Group (UK) Ltd, Croydon, CR0 4YY

16/04/2025

14658445-0001